Lumi Karmitsa

WILD MITTENS &
Unruly Socks

Search Press

This edition published in Great Britain in 2019 by
Search Press Ltd
Wellwood
North Farm Road
Tunbridge Wells
Kent TN2 3DR

Also published in the United States of America
in 2018 by Trafalgar Square Books
North Pomfret, Vermont, 05053

Originally published in Finnish as *Villit vanttuut & vallattomat villasukat.*

Patterns, drawings, and charts: Lumi Karmitsa
Photographs: Ritva Tuomi
Interior graphic design and layout: Sini Nihtilä
Translation into English: Maija van de Pavert
Cover design: RM Didier

ISBN: 978-1-78221-717-6

Suppliers
If you have difficulty in obtaining any of the materials and equipment mentioned in this book, please visit the Search Press website for details of suppliers: www.searchpress.com

Printed in China

WILD MITTENS &

Unruly Socks

CONTENTS

WILD MITTENS

WILD & Unruly

Unruly Socks

FOREWORD

A few years back, I decided to knit stranded mittens for a friend. I had taken craft classes at school and learned to knit and purl, and I had a pattern in front of me; the idea that I still might not be able to do it didn't even cross my mind. Why shouldn't I pull it off, when others could? The mittens turned out passable, and my friend still wears them. I've since encountered people in the internet knitting groups who've knitted for 45 years but never dared to try stranded knitting. I'm glad I hadn't heard such tales when I knitted my first mittens! Of course it's always going to be slower to work with two strands of yarn, but I'm pleased to be able to reassure you that stranded knitting isn't rocket science. In the end, all you need is courage. I decided to take my courage and run with it, and now I'm designing my own patterns. Here you have them, all my wild and unruly creations. I hope they bring joy to friends of stranded knitting everywhere, old and new! And especially that all of you who've trembled at the thought of stranded knitting, whether for 45 years or not, will pick up your needles and go for it.

Life is too short to knit with just one color!

Lumi Karmitsa

Kouvola, Finland

HOLDING YARNS:

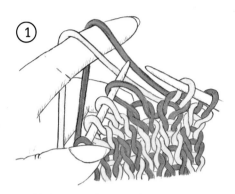

Hold the yarns always in the same order on your index finger.

Hold the dominant color closer to your work.

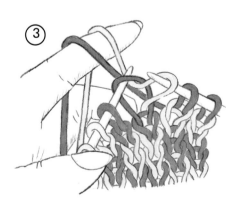

Hold the background color further from the work and cross the yarn over the dominant color when knitting.

How? What? Huh?—
A SHORT DESCRIPTION OF TECHNIQUES

All the socks and mittens in this book are knitted on five double-pointed needles from the cuff down. The charts have vertical lines at the needle change. Use a long tail cast-on unless pattern indicates otherwise.

Read the charts from right to left, bottom to top. If a sock pattern has a separate chart for the heel flap knitted flat, read it on the right side from right to left, on the wrong side left to right.

The patterns in this book use mainly yarns from Regia and Garnstudio DROPS, which are available from certain retailers (see Yarn Information on page 128) or can be substituted for with yarns of a similar weight and composition. You can adjust the size by changing needle size and/or yarn weight.

Stranded Knitting

Stranded knitting is stockinette knitting using two or more colors to form patterns. In most patterns, only two colors are used on each row, since using more colors than that tends to get very tricky.

There are many techniques to holding yarns (images 1–3), so it may be a good idea to try another technique if the one I'm showing doesn't feel natural. Some knitters use a yarn guide on one finger to hold the yarns.

More frequent color changes equals a neater fabric. However, most patterns in this book have large areas of single color, where the other color floats along behind the work. In this case, you have to catch the floats every 2–5 stitches. You should always catch them at a different place on different rows; otherwise, the catch points may show on the right side as ugly vertical lines.

CATCHING FLOATS BEHIND YOUR WORK

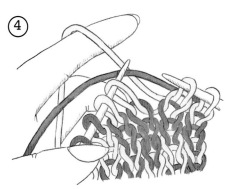

Lift the yarn you need to catch over the yarn you are knitting.

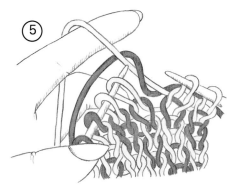

Pull the yarn you need to catch under the yarn you are knitting and back over it.

It's a good idea to alternate between the methods in 4 and 5 to avoid tangling the yarns. I personally always use the method in 4, because I find it neater—but on the other hand, doing it that way means that I'm frequently pausing to untangle my yarns. It's easy to untangle yarns when knitting small objects like socks or mittens: simply hold both yarns, lift your work in the air, and let it spin around and untangle itself. If you're using multiple balls of yarn but the others have not twisted with the two yarns you are currently knitting, you can tuck the extra balls inside your work and use the same method.

Stranded knitting doesn't yield a very stretchy fabric. For that reason, you should choose needles at least one size larger than you'd otherwise use with the yarn you've chosen. You can also stretch your work lightly after finishing a needle to avoid the floats drawing in your fabric.

Steaming

I know many knitters who couldn't care less for steaming. But it works wonders for stranded knitting. Some patterns benefit more than others; for example, Merry Skull Socks and Kittycats looked at first like a chimpanzee had tried its hand with stranded knitting, but after steaming I could have sold them in a store.

You need an iron and a muslin cloth (I use a thin kitchen towel) for steaming. Soak the cloth and place it on top of your knitting. Use the temperature recommended for your yarn and hold the iron on top of the cloth for a short while. Don't apply pressure or slide the iron as you normally would—a light touch is enough. After you've steamed the whole work, allow it to dry flat.

VERTICAL DUPLICATE STITCH:

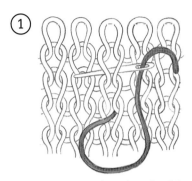

① Bring your yarn to the right side of the work at the bottom of the stitch you wish to cover. Pull the needle through the top of the stitch from right to left.

Duplicate Stitch

Duplicate stitch is handy when you want to add splashes of color into two-color stranded knitting. It can also be used to correct small mistakes in your work. You should use yarn the same weight as your knitting yarn.

HORIZONTAL DUPLICATE STITCH:

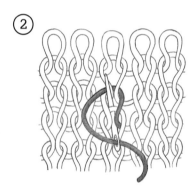

② Pull the needle to the wrong side of work at the bottom of the stitch and back up at the center of the stitch. Keep working this way along the column of stitches.

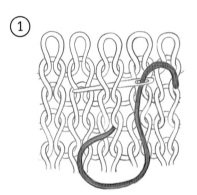

① Bring your yarn to the right side of the work at the bottom of the stitch you wish to cover. Pull the needle through the top of the stitch from right to left.

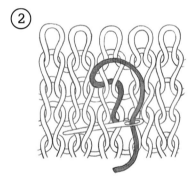

② Pull the needle to the wrong side of work at the bottom of the stitch and bring it back up at the bottom of the next stitch. Keep working this way along the row of stitches.

Knitted Cast On

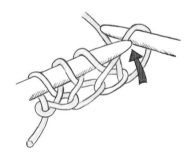

Start with a slip knot, as you would with a long-tail cast on. Slip the knot onto your left needle and place the working yarn on your index finger, just as you do when knitting. *Insert the right needle into the stitch on your left needle and pull through as if to knit. Do not slip the stitch off the left needle. Slide down the stitch you just made on your left needle as shown in the image.* Repeat * to * until you have the desired number of stitches.

Abbreviations

ST = stitch

K = knit

P = purl

KTBL = knit through back loop

YO = yarn over

K2TOG = knit 2 stitches together

K3TOG = knit 3 stitches together

P2TOG = purl 2 stitches together

SSK = Slip 2 stitches knitwise one by one onto your right needle. Return the stitches onto your left needle and knit them together through the back loop.

SSSK = Slip 3 stitches knitwise one by one onto your right needle. Return the stitches onto your left needle and knit them together through the back loop.

M1R = Lift the bar between stitches on your left needle from back to front. Knit the lifted stitch through the front loop. The stitch leans to the right.

M1L = Lift the bar between stitches on your left needle from front to back. Knit the lifted stitch through the back loop. The stitch leans to the left.

SLIP 1 KNITWISE = Insert your right needle into the stitch as if to knit and slip it into the right needle.

SLIP 1 PURLWISE = Insert your right needle into the stitch as if to purl and slip it into the right needle.

GAUGE = tension (UK)

·Mews·

·Tigers·

·Peonies·

·Giraffes·

WILD MITTENS

·Jesus Saves·

Buddhas

These Buddha mittens have a simple gussetless thumb. The easy twisted cuff is knitted flat.

SKILL LEVEL: Experienced
SIZE: Large women's size
YARN: CYCA #3 (DK/light worsted)
Regia 6-ply
150 g / 375 m, 75% virgin wool /
25% polyamide
– Color A natur (01992), approx. 35 g
– Color B pink (06345), approx. 15 g
– Color C weinrot (06046), approx.
30 g
Regia Active 6-ply 50 g / 125 m,
40% wool / 40% acrylic /
25% polyamide
– Color D green (05967), approx. 5 g
NEEDLES: Set of double pointed
needles, U. S. size 2.5 / 3 mm
GAUGE: 28 sts and 30 rows of
stranded knitting = 4 x 4 in /
10 x 10 cm. Adjust needle size to
obtain correct gauge if necessary.

B) THUMB (same for both hands)

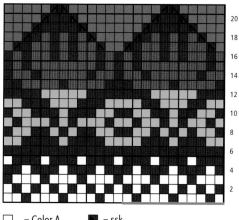

☐ = Color A   ◼ = ssk
▦ = Color B   ◪ = k2tog
■ = Color C   ▨ = no stitch
▥ = Color D

TWISTED CUFF: With Color A, cast on 60 sts and work 7 rows of stockinette stitch back and forth. **Next row (RS):** K5 and twist the left needle once around itself towards you to twist your work. Continue to knit and repeat the twist every 5 sts until the end of the row.

Divide the stitches onto 4 needles (15 sts / needle) and join to work in the round. With Color A, k 1 row and p 1 row. Begin stranded knitting following Chart A. **Note:** Each hand has its own chart.

On Row 30 of Chart A, place your thumb stitches on a scrap yarn. Here's how to do it: K11 with a contrasting scrap yarn at the place shown in the chart. Slide these stitches back onto your left needle and continue the pattern with your working yarns. The scrap yarn is where your thumb will be. Continue in pattern until you have reached the top of Chart A.

With 8 sts remaining, cut the yarn and pull through stitches. Pull tight.

THUMB: Remove the scrap yarn and at the same time pick up the stitches from the bottom and top of the gap. Pick up an additional stitch from each end of the gap. You now have 24 sts. Divide them onto 3 needles. Begin stranded knitting following Chart B for thumbs. Start at the right side of the bottom of the thumb (same chart for both thumbs). Finish off with decreases following the chart. With 4 sts remaining, cut the yarn and pull through stitches. Pull tight. If there are any holes at the start of the thumb, you can carefully sew them shut when weaving in ends.

Weave in ends on the wrong side and sew the cuff seam. Steam press the mittens lightly.

A) RIGHT HAND

	= Color A		= purl
	= Color B		= ssk
	= Color C		= k2tog
	= Color D		= no stitch

A) LEFT HAND

□ = Color A	■ = purl
▨ = Color B	◩ = ssk
■ = Color C	◪ = k2tog
▨ = Color D	▨ = no stitch

Peonies ·

You should choose a dark color for the main color of Peonies. This will make the long floats less visible. You can play more with colors in the fulled Peonies (see page 24), since the caught floats won't be as visible in the fulled fabric.

SKILL LEVEL: Experienced
SIZE: Large women's size
YARN: CYCA #3 (DK/light worsted)
Drops Karisma
50 g / 100 m, 100% wool
– Color A black (05), approx. 65 g
– Color B white (19), approx. 30 g
NEEDLES: Set of double-pointed needles, U. S. size 2.5 / 3 mm for cuff and U. S. size 4 / 3.5 mm for stranded knitting
GAUGE: 24 sts and 26 rows of stranded knitting = 4 x 4 in / 10 x 10 cm. Adjust needle size to obtain correct gauge if necessary.

With Color A and smaller needles, cast on 52 sts (13 sts / needle) and join to work in the round. Work k2, p2 ribbing for 8 rows. K 1 row. Change to larger needles and begin stranded knitting following Chart A. **Note:** Each hand has its own chart. Follow Chart B for thumb gusset at the red squares. **Note:** Each gusset has its own chart. Make sure you don't catch the yarn where you increase next round to avoid floats being visible on the right side. Once the gusset chart is complete, work in pattern until you reach the gusset. Slip the 15 gusset stitches onto scrap yarn. Cast on 1 st across the gap and continue Chart A until the end of row 46.

TIP: To make the tip just as warm as the rest of the mitten and keep your gauge consistent, knit with two strands of Color A held together. Take one yarn end from the outside and the other from the inside of the ball. Decrease as indicated in the chart. With 8 sts remaining, cut yarns, pull one through the stitches, and pull tight.

THUMB: With Color A, work the thumb in the same manner as the tip. Pick up the stitches on the scrap yarn and pick up and knit 5 additional sts across the gap. Divide these 20 sts onto 3 larger needles and knit with two strands held together for 13 rows. Cut the other yarn. Continue with one strand, *k2tog*. Repeat * to * until the end of the row. K 1 row. *K2tog*. Repeat * to * until the end of the row. You have 5 sts remaining. Cut the yarn, pull through the stitches and pull tight.

Weave in ends and steam press the mittens lightly.

➤

B) RIGHT GUSSET

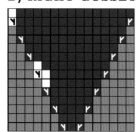

■ = no stitch
◢ = k2tog
◣ = ssk
◥ = M1r
◤ = M1l

A) RIGHT HAND

■ = Color A
□ = Color B

B) LEFT GUSSET

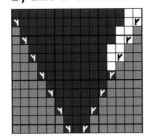

- ▨ = no stitch
- ◪ = k2tog
- ◩ = ssk
- ⊮ = M1r
- ⊯ = M1l

A) LEFT HAND

■ = Color A
□ = Color B

· Fulled Peonies ·

SKILL LEVEL: Experienced
SIZE: Medium women's size
YARN: CYCA #5 (chunky/craft/rug)
Novita Joki
50 g / 105 m, 100 % wool
– Color A black (099), approx. 75 g
– Color B off-white (010), approx. 40 g
OR
– Color A off-white (010), approx. 75 g
– Color B variegated heather (859), approx.
40 g
NEEDLES: Set of double-pointed needles,
U. S. size 10 / 6 mm
GAUGE: 18 sts and 17 rows of stranded
knitting = 4 x 4 in / 10 x 10 cm. Adjust needle
size to obtain correct gauge if necessary.
**WIDTH OF THE MITTEN ABOVE THE
THUMB BEFORE FULLING:** approx.
6 in / 15 cm
**LENGTH OF THE MITTEN BEFORE
FULLING:** approx. 14 in / 36 cm

With Color A, cast on 52 sts (13 sts / needle) and join to work in the round. P 1 row and k 7 rows. Begin stranded knitting following Chart A. **Note:** Each hand has its own chart. Follow Chart B for gusset at the red squares. **Note:** Each gusset has its own chart. Once the gusset is finished, knit in pattern until you reach the gusset. Slip the 15 gusset stitches onto scrap yarn. Cast on 1 st across the gap and continue Chart A until the end of Row 47.

Follow the instructions below for decreases, not the chart:
1st decrease row: *K3, k2tog*. Repeat * to * until 2 sts remain, k2.
K 3 rows.

2nd decrease row: *K2, k2tog*. Repeat * to * until 2 sts remain, k2.
K 2 rows.
3rd decrease row: *K1, k2tog*. Repeat * to * until 1 st remains, k1.
K 1 row.
4th decrease row: *K2tog*. Repeat * to * until 1 st remains, k1.
5th decrease row: *K2tog*. Repeat * to * until 1 st remains, k1.

You have 6 sts remaining. Cut the yarn, pull through the stitches and pull tight.

THUMB: With Color A, pick up the stitches on the scrap yarn and pick up and knit 5 additional stitches across the gap. Divide these 20 sts onto 3 needles and knit in the round for 13 rows.
Next row: *k2tog*, repeat * to * until the end of the row.
Next row: Knit.
Next row: *k2tog*, repeat * to * until the end of the row. You have 5 sts remaining. Cut the yarn, pull through the stitches and pull tight. Weave in ends.

FULLING: Insert a small plastic bag inside the thumb and secure it with a few stitches to avoid fulling the thumb solid. Insert another plastic bag into the tip of the mitten and attach similarly. Put the mittens in the washing machine with a couple of towels. Select a hot wash program that lasts for about an hour (normal spin cycle, no prewash). Regular detergent can be used if you want. Stretch the mittens to correct size after the wash. If the thumbs seem a bit too big, put the mitten on your hand and rub it under warm running water until it's the right size. Let dry. Next time you can wash the mittens the same way as other wool garments.

· Mews ·

These Mew mittens have a thumb gusset and an easy twisted cuff that's knitted back and forth.

SKILL LEVEL: Experienced
SIZE: Medium women's size
YARN: CYCA #2 (sport/baby)
Drops Fabel
50 g / 205 m, 75% wool / 25% polyamide
– Color A pink (102), approx. 30 g
– Color B off-white (100), approx. 25 g
NEEDLES: Set of double-pointed needles, U. S. size 2.5 / 3 mm
GAUGE: 32 sts and 33 rows of stranded knitting = 4 x 4 in / 10 x 10 cm. Adjust needle size to obtain correct gauge if necessary.

TWISTED CUFF: With Color B, cast on 60 sts and work 6 rows of garter stitch back and forth. **Next row (WS):** K5, twist the left needle once around itself towards you to twist your work. Continue to knit and repeat the twist every 5 stitches until the end of the row.

Join to work in the round and p 1 row with Color B. Cut the yarn and continue with Color A. K 1 row, work 8 rows of k1tbl, p2 ribbing, k 1 row, p 2 rows and k 1 row. Work k2, p2 ribbing for 14 rows. On the final ribbing row, inc 1 st on each needle. You now have 64 sts.

K 1 row. Then begin stranded knitting following Chart A. Divide onto needles as indicated by vertical lines. Follow Chart B to work the thumb gusset at the black squares (both mittens have the same thumb). Once the gusset is complete, knit in pattern until 1 st before the gusset starts. Slip that 1 stitch, 13 gusset sts, and 1 st after the gusset onto scrap yarn. Cast on 3 sts across the gap and continue Chart A. With 12 sts remaining, cut yarn, pull through the stitches, and pull tight.

THUMB: Pick up the stitches on the scrap yarn. Following Thumb Chart B, pick up and knit an additional 11 sts across the gap. Divide all 26 sts onto 3 needles and continue Row 1 of Chart B. Slip the last stitch of row 1 onto Ndl 1; it is now the first stitch of Row 2. Continue working in the round following Chart B until you have 6 sts remaining. Cut yarn, pull through stitches, and pull tight.

Weave in ends on the wrong side and sew the cuff seam. Steam press the mittens lightly.

➡

In Finnish, cats make a slightly different sound! The chart has been updated for English-speaking cats.

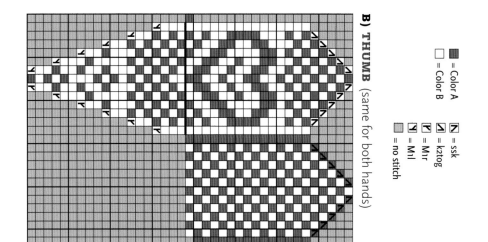

= Color A
= Color B
↘ = ssk
↗ = k2tog
↖ = M1r
↙ = M1l
= no stitch

B) THUMB (same for both hands)

A) RIGHT HAND

2 4 6 8 10 12 14 16 18 20 22 24 26 28 30 32 34 36 38 40 42 44 46 48 50 52 54 56 58 60 62

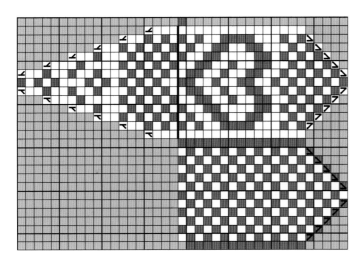

Giraffes

The gusseted thumb of Giraffes blends into the animal pattern almost seamlessly. To make the cuff neater, you may want to fold it in half and attach onto the wrong side.

SKILL LEVEL: Experienced
SIZE: Medium women's size
YARN: CYCA #2 (sport/baby)
Drops Fabel
50 g / 205 m, 75% wool /
25% polyamide
– Color A off-white (100), approx.
30 g
– Color B mustard yellow (111),
approx. 25 g
NEEDLES: Set of double-pointed
needles, U. S. size 1.5 / 2.5 mm for
cuff and 2.5 / 3 mm for stranded
knitting
GAUGE: 32 sts and 33 rows of
stranded knitting = 4 x 4 in /
10 x 10 cm. Adjust needle size to
obtain correct gauge if necessary.

With Color A and smaller needles, cast on 64 sts (16 sts / needle) and join to work in the round. Work k2, p2 ribbing for 20 rows. K 1 row. Change to larger needles and begin stranded knitting following Chart A. **Note:** Each hand has its own chart. Divide stitches onto needles as indicated by vertical lines. Follow Chart B to work the thumb gusset at the black squares. Once the gusset is complete, knit in pattern until 1 st before the gusset begins. Slip that 1 stitch, 13 gusset sts, and 1 st after the gusset onto scrap yarn. Cast on 3 sts across the gap and continue Chart A. With 12 sts remaining, cut yarn, pull through the stitches and pull tight.

THUMB: Pick up the stitches on scrap yarn with larger needles. Following Thumb Chart B, pick up and knit an additional 9 sts across the gap. Divide these 24 sts onto 3 needles and knit in the round following Chart B until you have 6 sts remaining. Cut yarn and pull through stitches. Pull tight.

Weave in ends on the wrong side of work. You may want to fold the cuff and attach it to the wrong side to make the cuff neater. Steam press the mittens lightly.

B) RIGHT THUMB

A) RIGHT HAND

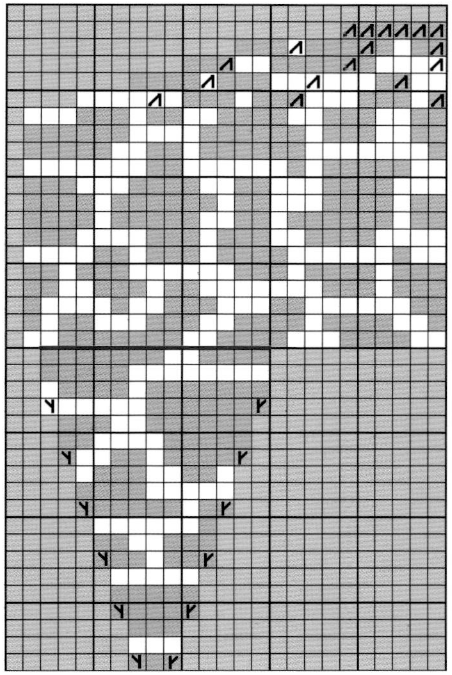

□ = Color A
▨ = Color B

◪ = ssk
◩ = k2tog
◩ = M1r
◪ = M1l
▨ = no stitch

32

B) LEFT THUMB

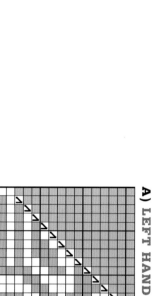

A) LEFT HAND

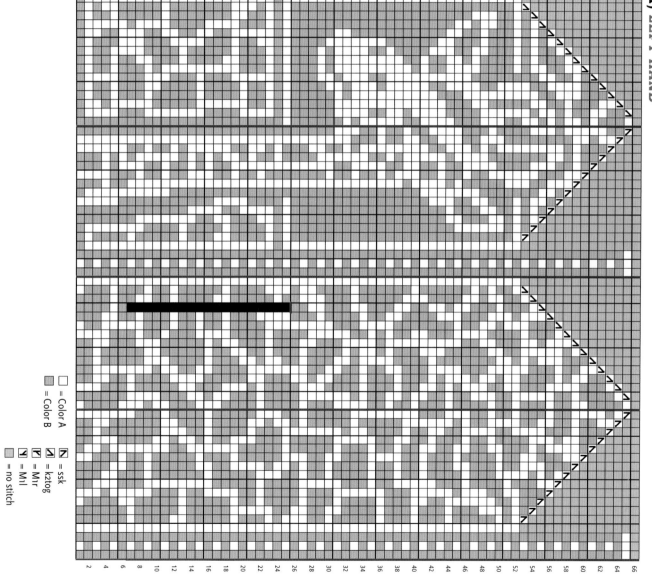

□ = Color A
▨ = Color B

N = ssk
⊿ = k2tog
⊮ = M1r
⊯ = M1l
▨ = no stitch

NOTE:

Each mitten has its own chart! The pattern for Capitalist's Wrist Warmers is on page 38.

Capitalist's Mittens

These money-themed mittens incorporate a snug "Indian" or "lifeline" thumb gusset. This pattern is a breeze to knit, since there are no long floats except on a few rows at the beginning and the end. The repetitive pattern is also easy to memorize.

SKILL LEVEL: Experienced
SIZE: Medium women's size
YARN: CYCA #2 (sport/baby) Drops Fabel
50 g / 205 m, 75% wool / 25% polyamide
– Color A gray (200), approx. 35 g
CYCA #1 (sock/fingering/baby)
Regia Fluormania Color 4-ply
100 g / 410 m, 75% wool / 25% polyamide
– Color B neon rainbow color (07188),
approx. 30 g
NEEDLES: Set of double-pointed needles,
U. S. size 0 / 2 mm for cuff and 1.5 / 2.5 mm
for stranded knitting
GAUGE: 35 sts and 35 rows of stranded
knitting = 4 x 4 in / 10 x 10 cm. Adjust needle size to obtain correct gauge if necessary.

With Color A and smaller needles, cast on 64 sts (16 sts / needle). Join to work in the round. Work k2, p2 ribbing for 20 rows. K 2 more rows. Change to larger needles and begin stranded knitting following Chart A. Divide onto needles as indicated by vertical lines.

RIGHT HAND: At the end of Chart A, transfer the stitches on Ndl 3 (24 sts) onto scrap yarn. Transfer half of the stitches on Ndl 4 to Ndl 3. You now have 16 sts on each needle. Continue working in the round following Chart B. When you have reached the last row of Chart B, knit until 4 sts remain. Transfer them to Ndl 1. This is the new beginning of row. Transfer 4 sts from Ndl 1 to Ndl 2, 4 sts from Ndl 2 to Ndl 3, and 4 sts from Ndl 3 to Ndl 4. You now have 16 sts on each needle. Continue to Chart C.

LEFT HAND: At the end of Chart A, transfer the stitches on Ndl 2 (24 sts) onto scrap yarn. Transfer half of the stitches on Ndl 1 to Ndl 2. You now have 16 sts on each needle. Continue knitting in the round following Chart B. At the end of Chart B, knit the additional 4 sts on the Chart from Ndl 1 onto Ndl 4. This is the new beginning of row. Transfer 4 sts from Ndl 2 to Ndl 1, 4 sts from Ndl 3 to Ndl 2, and 4 sts from Ndl 4 to Ndl 3. You now have 16 sts on each needle. Continue to Chart C.

After you have finished the decreases on Chart C, you have 8 sts remaining. Cut yarn and pull through the stitches. Pull tight.

THUMB: Pick up the stitches on scrap yarn with smaller needles, and pick up and knit an additional 5 sts across the gap with Color A. Divide these 29 sts onto 3 needles. Begin stranded knitting following Row 1 of Chart D. With 7 sts remaining, cut yarn, pull through the stitches, and pull tight.

Weave in ends and steam press the mittens lightly.

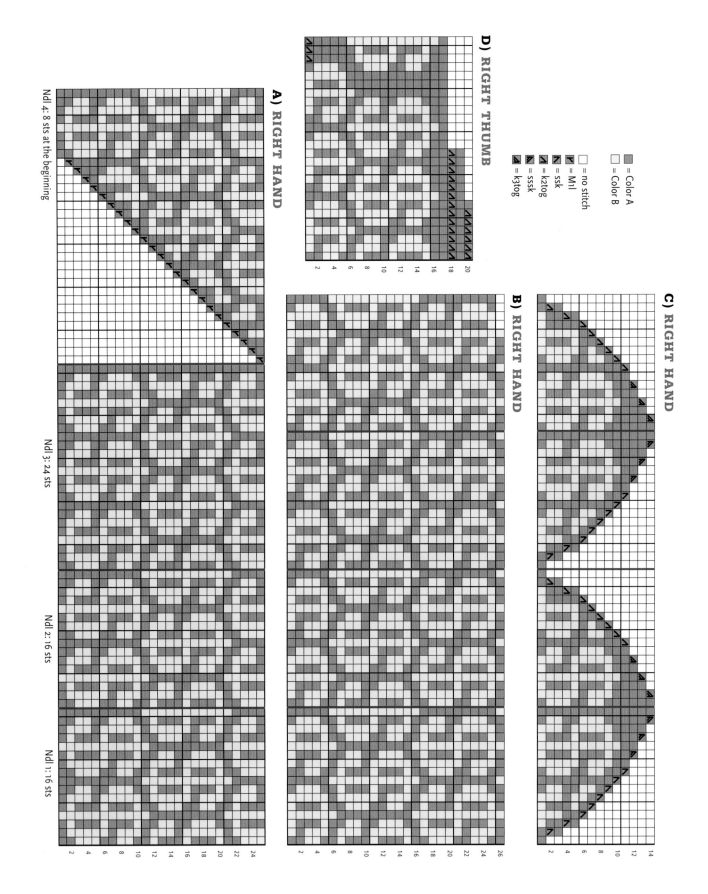

D) RIGHT THUMB

= Color A
= Color B
= no stitch
= M1
= ssk
= k2tog
= sssk
= k3tog

A) RIGHT HAND

B) RIGHT HAND

C) RIGHT HAND

Ndl 4: 8 sts at the beginning

Ndl 3: 24 sts

Ndl 2: 16 sts

Ndl 1: 16 sts

WILD MITTENS

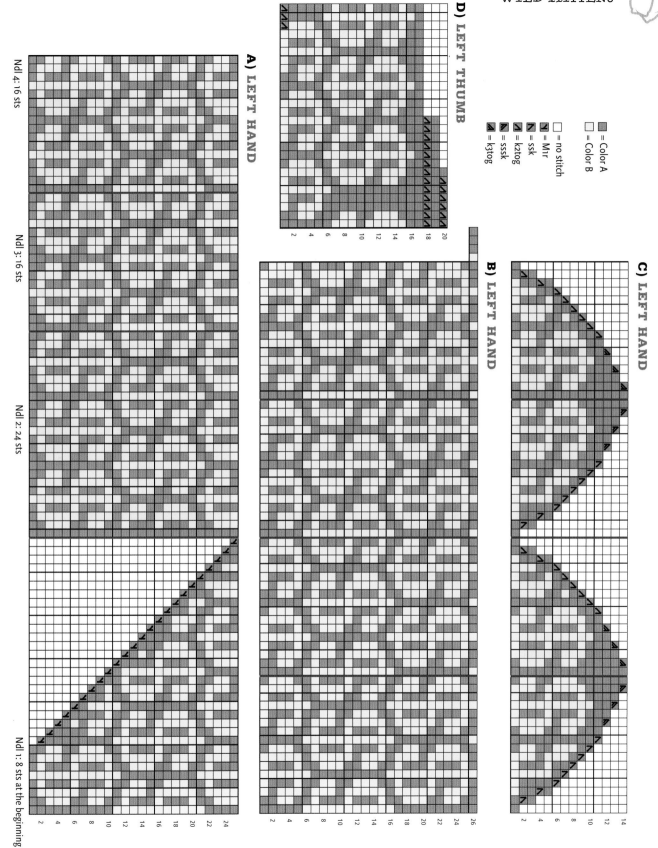

D) LEFT THUMB

= Color A
= Color B
= no stitch
= M1r
= ssk
= k2tog
= sssk
= k3tog

A) LEFT HAND

B) LEFT HAND

C) LEFT HAND

Ndl 4: 16 sts

Ndl 3: 16 sts

Ndl 2: 24 sts

Ndl 1: 8 sts at the beginning

Capitalist's Wrist Warmers

SKILL LEVEL: Experienced
SIZE: Medium women's size
YARN: CYCA #1 (sock/fingering/baby) Regia 4-ply
50 g / 210 m, 75% wool / 25% polyamide
– Color A dark gray (00522), approx. 25 g
CYCA #1 (sock/fingering/baby) Regia Fluormania Color 4-ply
100 g / 410 m, 75% wool / 25% polyamide
– Color B neon rainbow color (07188), approx. 15 g
NEEDLES: Set of double-pointed needles, U. S. size 0 / 2 mm for cuff and 1.5 / 2.5 mm for stranded knitting
GAUGE: 35 sts and 35 rows of stranded knitting = 4 x 4 in / 10 x 10 cm. Adjust needle size to obtain correct gauge if necessary.

Follow the Capitalist's Mittens pattern until the end of Row 5 of Chart B. Work one more round, but use CC only for the tips of $ signs you have already knitted, and don't start a new row of $ signs. Change to smaller needles; k 1 row with Color A. Work k2, p2 ribbing for 10 rows. Use basic bind off to bind off your stitches.

THUMB: Follow the Capitalist's Mittens pattern until the end of Row 5 of Thumb Chart D. Work one more round, but use Color B only for the tips of dollar signs you've already knitted—don't start a new row of dollar signs. Change to smaller needles and k 1 row with Color A. Work k2, p2 ribbing for 5 rows. Decrease 2 sts on the first ribbing row. Use basic bind off to bind off your stitches.

Weave in ends and steam press the mittens lightly.

You should choose a dark color for the main color of Tigers. This will make the long floats less visible. The mittens incorporate a gusseted thumb, and the eyes of the tiger are added with duplicate stitch.

SKILL LEVEL: Experienced
SIZE: Large women's size
YARN: CYCA #3 (DK/light worsted) Drops Karisma
50 g / 100 m, 100% wool
– Color A black (05), approx. 60 g
– Color B white (19), approx. 15 g
– Color C orange (11), approx. 25 g
– Color D sea green (50), a small amount for eyes
NEEDLES: Set of double-pointed needles, U. S. size 2.5 / 3 mm for cuff and size 4 / 3.5 mm for stranded knitting
GAUGE: 24 sts and 26 rows of stranded knitting = 4 x 4 in / 10 x 10 cm. Adjust needle size to obtain correct gauge if necessary.

With Color A and smaller needles, cast on 52 sts (13 sts / needle) and join to work in the round. Work k2, p2 ribbing for 8 rows. K 1 row. Change to larger needles and begin stranded knitting following Chart A.
Note: Each hand has its own chart.

At the green square on Row 11 of Chart A, begin the gusset increases as follows: M1r, k1, M1l. Continue stranded knitting in pattern and make gusset increases at the green square every other row 7 times in total. Two gusset stitches are increased on each increase row. Make sure you don't catch the yarn where you increase on the next round to avoid floats being visible on the right side. K 1 row after the 7th increase row. The gusset is now complete. **Next row:** Knit in pattern until the beginning of the gusset. Slip the 15 gusset sts onto scrap yarn. Cast on 1 st across the gap and continue Chart A until you start decreasing.

The tiger's eyes are easiest to make now, when the mitten is still open at the tip. Use duplicate stitch to work the eyes (see page 10). With black yarn, work over the black stitches around the eye in duplicate stitch, too, to make it all really pop. Weave in ends before beginning decreases.

Decrease as indicated on the chart. With 8 sts remaining, cut yarn, pull through the stitches, and pull tight.

THUMB: To make the thumb as warm as the rest of the mitten, knit with two strands of Color A held together. Take one yarn end from the outside and the other from the inside of the ball.

Pick up the stitches on the scrap yarn and pick up and knit 5 additional sts across the gap. Divide these 20 sts onto 3 larger needles and knit with two strands held together for 13 rows. Cut one strand.

Next row: Continue with one strand and *k2tog*. Repeat * to * until the end of the row.

Next row: Knit.

Next row: *k2tog*; repeat * to * until the end of the row.

You have 5 sts remaining. Cut the yarn, pull through the stitches, and pull tight.

Weave in ends and steam press the mittens lightly.

RIGHT HAND

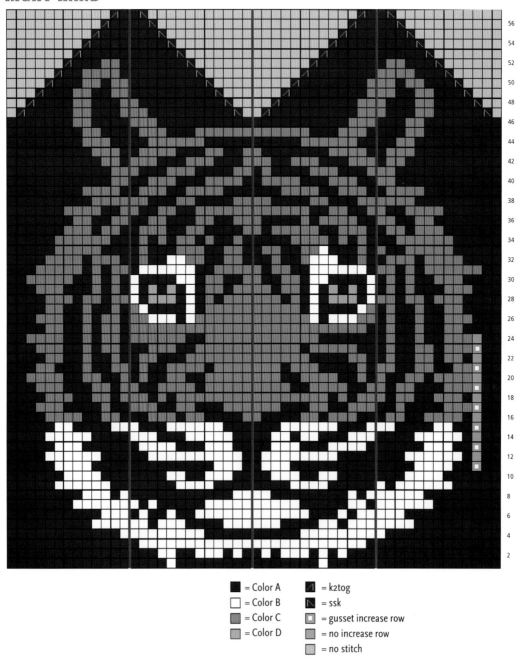

	= Color A		= k2tog
	= Color B		= ssk
	= Color C		= gusset increase row
	= Color D		= no increase row
			= no stitch

LEFT HAND

■ = Color A   ◪ = k2tog
□ = Color B   ◩ = ssk
▦ = Color C   ▫ = gusset increase row
▨ = Color D   ▪ = no increase row
               ▨ = no stitch

·London Calling·

These mittens incorporate a gusseted thumb and a wedge tip. The pattern uses three colors for a few rows—the faces of the guards—but otherwise it's two-color stranded knitting throughout. If weaving in ends isn't your favorite pastime, you can try a self-striping yarn instead of Colors A, B, and C.

SKILL LEVEL: Experienced
SIZE: Large women's size
YARN: CYCA #3 (DK/light worsted)
Drops Karisma
50 g / 100 m, 100% wool
– for ribbing, navy blue (17), approx. 25 g
– Color A bright blue (07), approx. 15 g
– Color B light sky blue (68), approx. 15 g
– Color C white (19), approx. 20 g
– Color D red (18), approx. 25 g
– Color E black (05), approx. 10 g
– Color F light oak (77), a small amount
NEEDLES: Set of double-pointed needles,
U. S. size 2.5 / 3 mm for ribbing and size 4 /
3.5 mm for stranded knitting
GAUGE: 24 sts and 26 rows of stranded
knitting = 4 x 4 in / 10 x 10 cm. Adjust nee-
dle size to obtain correct gauge if necessary.

SIZE: Children's (approx. 5 years)
YARN: CYCA #1 (sock/fingering/baby)
Regia 4-ply
50 g / 210 m, 75% wool / 25% polyamide
– for ribbing, dark blue (00324), approx. 10 g
– Color A blue (02137), approx. 5 g
– Color B light blue (01980), approx. 10g
– Color C pearl grey (01991), approx. 10 g
– Color D red (02054), approx. 10 g
– Color E black (02066), approx. 5 g
– Color F light brown (00017), a small amount
NEEDLES: Set of double-pointed needles,
U. S. size 1.5 / 2.5 mm for ribbing and size
2.5 / 3 mm for stranded knitting
GAUGE: 32 sts and 33 rows of stranded
knitting = 4 x 4 in / 10 x 10 cm. Adjust nee-
dle size to obtain correct gauge if necessary.

With ribbing color and smaller needles, cast on 50 sts (12 sts / 13 sts / 12 sts / 13 sts) and join to work in the round. P 2 rows and k 1 row. Work k1tbl, p1 ribbing for 15 rows. K 1 row and p 2 rows.

Change to larger needles and begin stranded knitting following the chart. **Note:** Each hand has its own chart. At the yellow square on Row 7 of the chart, begin the gusset increases as follows: M1r, k 1, M1l. Continue stranded knitting in pattern and make gusset increases at the yellow square every other row—7 times in total. Two gusset stitches are increased on each increase row. Use Color A, B, or C for gusset stitches on chart rows worked in those colors, with Color D always floating at the back of the work. Make sure you don't catch the yarn where you increase on the next round to avoid floats being visible on the right side.

Once the gusset is complete, knit the next row in pattern until you reach the gusset. Slip the 15 gusset sts onto scrap yarn. Cast on 1 st across the gap and continue the chart until you start decreasing.

Decrease as indicated on the chart. With 6 sts remaining, cut yarn, pull through the stitches, and pull tight.

THUMB: Use Color C for thumb. Pick up the stitches on the scrap yarn with smaller needles, and pick up and knit 3 additional sts across the gap. Divide these 18 sts onto 3 needles and knit in the round for 13 rows, or until your thumb is almost covered.

Next row: *K2tog*, repeat * to * until the end of the row.

Next row: Knit.

Next row: *K2tog*, repeat * to * until 1 st remains, k1.

You have 5 sts remaining. Cut the yarn, pull through the stitches, and pull tight. If there are any holes at the start of the thumb, sew them closed when weaving in ends.

Weave in ends and steam press the mittens lightly.

LEFT HAND

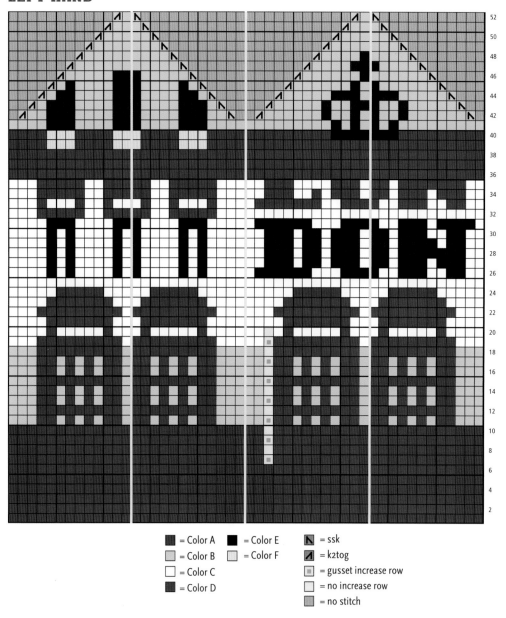

■ = Color A ■ = Color E ◣ = ssk
▨ = Color B ▨ = Color F ◢ = k2tog
□ = Color C ▪ = gusset increase row
■ = Color D □ = no increase row
▨ = no stitch

46

RIGHT HAND

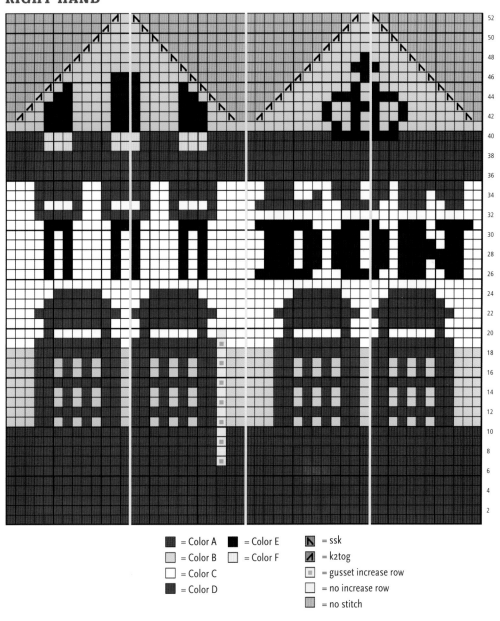

	= Color A		= Color E	= ssk
	= Color B		= Color F		= k2tog
	= Color C				= gusset increase row
	= Color D				= no increase row
					= no stitch

·Jesus Saves·

This laughing Jesus saves early and often! The mittens incorporate a gusseted thumb with Christian symbols of faith, hope, and love. It's fine to use only two colors instead of three at the cuff and the tip, if you prefer.

SKILL LEVEL: Experienced
SIZE: Medium women's size
YARNS FOR RETRO COLOR SET:
CYCA #1 (sock/fingering/baby)
Regia Design Line
100 g / 420 m, 75% wool / 25% polyamide
– Color A "Shadow Stripe" by Kaffe
Fassett (03871), approx. 20 g
CYCA #1 (sock/fingering/baby)
Regia 4-ply
50 g / 210 m, 75% wool / 25% polyamide
– Color B camel heather (00017), approx.
30 g
– Color C red heather (02742), approx. 10 g
– Color D marine (00324), approx. 20 g
YARNS FOR HIPPIE COLOR SET:
CYCA #1 (sock/fingering/baby) Schoppel
Wolle Zauberball
100 g / 420 m, 75% wool / 25% polyamide
– Color A, C, and D tropical fish (1564),
approx. 35 g
(For Color C, I made sure I had a color
repeat with the highest contrast possible
with Color B; but if you don't want to cut
the yarn and rejoin it, you can use some
other yarn instead.)
CYCA #2 (sport/baby) Drops Fabel
50 g / 205 m, 75% wool / 25% polyamide
– Color B off-white (100), approx. 25 g
NEEDLES: Set of double-pointed needles, U. S. size 1.5 / 2.5 mm for ribbing
and 2.5 / 3 mm for stranded knitting
GAUGE: 32 sts and 33 rows of stranded
knitting = 4 x 4 in / 10 x 10 cm. Adjust
needle size to obtain correct gauge if
necessary.

With Color A and smaller needles, cast on 64 sts (16 sts / needle) and join to work in the round. K 1 row, work 8 rows of k1tbl, p1 ribbing, k 1 row, p 1 row, k 1 row. Change to larger needles and begin stranded knitting following Chart A. **Note:** Each hand has its own chart. Follow Chart B to work the thumb gusset at the blue squares. Once the gusset is complete, knit in pattern until 1 st before the gusset begins. Slip that 1 stitch, 13 gusset sts, and 1 st after the gusset onto scrap yarn. Cast on 3 sts across the gap and continue knitting Chart A. With 12 sts remaining, cut yarn, pull through the stitches, and pull tight.

THUMB: Pick up the stitches on scrap yarn with larger needles. With Color C, pick up and knit 11 sts across the gap. Divide these 26 sts onto 3 needles and work in the round following Chart B until you have 7 sts remaining. Cut yarn, pull through stitches, and pull tight.

Weave in ends and steam press the mittens lightly.

2 4 6 8 10 12 14 16 18 20 22 24 26 28 30 32 34 36 38 40 42 44 46 48 50 52 54 56 58 60 62 64 66 68 70 72 74 76 78 80

= Color A
= Color B
= Color C
= Color D

= ssk
= k2tog
= sssk
= k3tog
= no stitch
= M1r
= M1l

B) THUMB (same for both hands)

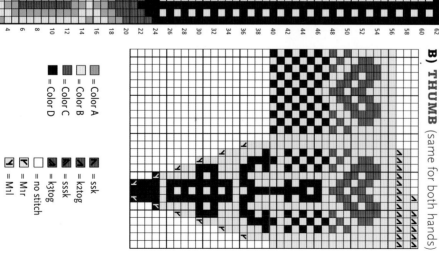

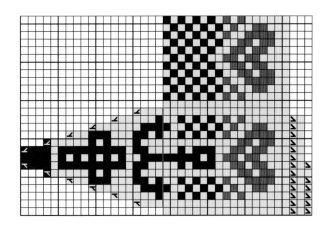

A) LEFT HAND

2 4 6 8 10 12 14 16 18 20 22 24 26 28 30 32 34 36 38 40 42 44 46 48 50 52 54 56 58 60 62 64 66 68 70 72 74 76 78 80

Chihuahua

WILD & unruly

merry skull

· MITTENS AND SOCKS ·

·merry skull mittens·

I challenge you to knit these mittens without cracking a smile. I bet you can't make it!

SKILL LEVEL: Experienced
SIZE: Medium men's size
YARN: CYCA #3 (DK/light worsted)
Regia 6-ply
150 g / 375 m, 75% virgin wool / 25%
polyamide
– Color A black (02066), approx. 50 g
– Color B white (06860), approx. 35 g
NEEDLES: Set of double-pointed
needles, U. S. size 2.5 / 3 mm
GAUGE: 28 sts and 30 rows of stranded
knitting = 4 x 4 in / 10 x 10 cm. Adjust
needle size to obtain correct gauge if
necessary.

SIZE: Medium women's size
YARN: CYCA #1 (sock/fingering/baby)
Regia 4-ply
50 g / 210 m, 75% wool / 25% polyamide
– Color A denim (02137), approx. 35 g
– Color B white (01992), approx. 20 g
NEEDLES: Set of double-pointed
needles, U. S. size 2.5 / 3 mm
GAUGE: 32 sts and 33 rows of stranded
knitting = 4 x 4 in / 10 x 10 cm. Adjust
needle size to obtain correct gauge if
necessary.

With Color A, cast on 64 sts and divide onto 4 needles (16 sts / needle). Join to work in the round. Work k2, p2 ribbing for 20 rows. K 1 row and increase 2 sts. You now have 66 sts. Begin stranded knitting following Chart A and divide stitches onto needles as indicated by the vertical lines. **Note:** Each hand has its own chart.

On Row 22 of the chart, place your thumb stitches onto scrap yarn. Here's how to do it: K12 with contrasting scrap yarn as shown on the chart. Return these stitches back onto your left needle and continue the pattern with your working yarns. The scrap yarn is where your thumb will be. Continue in pattern until you've reached the top of Chart A.

With 10 sts remaining, cut the yarn and pull through stitches. Pull tight.

THUMB: Remove the scrap yarn and at the same time pick up the stitches from the bottom and top of the gap. Pick up an additional 2 sts from both ends of the gap. You now have 28 sts. Divide these sts onto

3 needles and begin Thumb Chart B. **Note:** Each thumb has its own chart.

The beginning of the left thumb is the first stitch that was on the scrap yarn, and the beginning of the right thumb is the right top side at the additional picked-up stitches. Finish off with decreases following the chart. With 8 sts remaining, cut yarn, pull through the stitches, and pull tight. If there are any holes at the start of the thumb, you can carefully sew them shut when weaving in ends.

Weave in ends and steam press the mittens lightly.

■ = Color A	◪ = k2tog
☐ = Color B	◩ = ssk
	▤ = no stitch
	◪ = k3tog
	◩ = sssk

A) RIGHT HAND

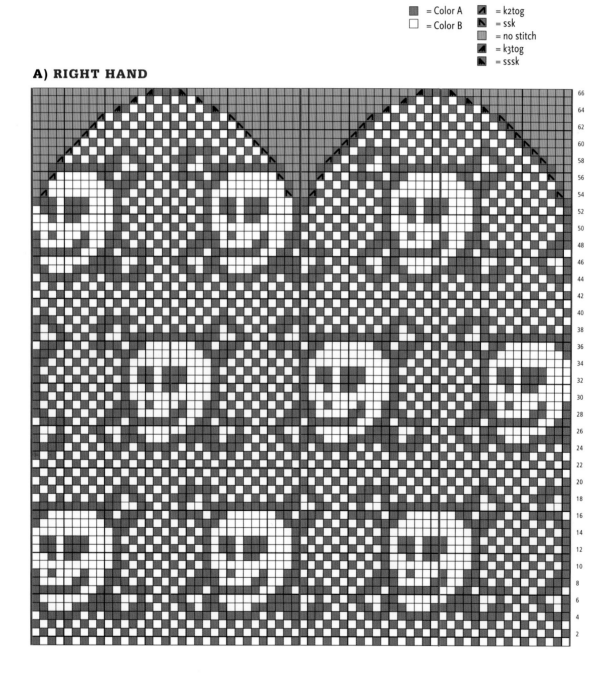

B) LEFT THUMB

B) RIGHT THUMB

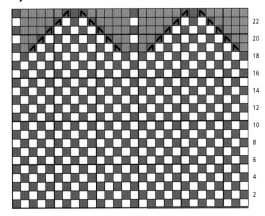
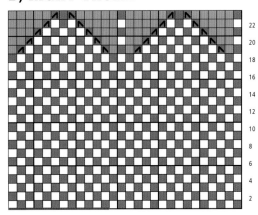

A) LEFT HAND

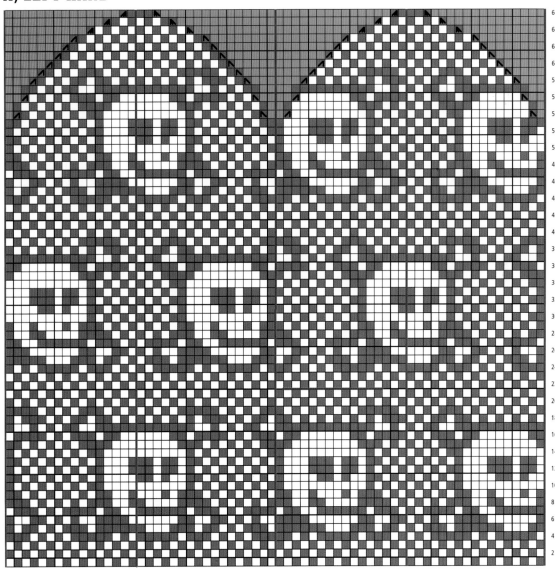

Merry Skull Socks

These Merry Skull Socks incorporate a reinforced French heel and a wedge toe. The gusset decreases are placed under the foot. You can choose to make either long socks or regular ones. There's no shaping at the leg part of the sock, so these are a better fit for people with narrow calves!

SKILL LEVEL: Experienced
SIZE: U. S. 7.5 / European 38
YARN FOR LONG SOCKS:
CYCA #2 (export/baby) Gjestal Maija
50 g / 130 m, 85% wool / 15 % polyamide
– Color A green (211), approx. 85 g
– Color B white (202), approx. 55 g
YARN FOR REGULAR SOCKS:
CYCA #2 (export/baby) Gjestal Maija
50 g / 130 m, 85% wool / 15% polyamide
– Color A ochra (218), approx. 70 g
– Color B white (202), approx. 40 g
NEEDLES: Set of double-pointed needles, U. S. size 1.5 / 2.5 mm for ribbing and 2.5 / 3 mm for stranded knitting
GAUGE: 28 sts and 30 rows = 4 x 4 in / 10 x 10 cm of stranded knitting. Adjust needle size to obtain correct gauge if necessary.

W ith Color A and smaller needles, cast on 64 sts (16 sts / needle) and join to work in the round. Work k2, p2 ribbing for 10 rows. Increase 2 sts on the last row of ribbing. You now have 66 sts. With Color A, k 1 row. Change to larger needles and begin stranded knitting following Row 1 of Chart A for long socks or Row 21 of Chart A for regular socks. **Note:** Each sock has its own chart. Divide the stitches onto the needles as indicated by vertical lines.

On Row 61 of Chart A, knit the sts on Ndl 1 onto Ndl 4. These 33 sts are used for the heel. Cut Color B, and use Color A for the heel.

HEEL FLAP: Turn work, p33. Turn work.
Row 1: K2, *slip 1, k1*. Repeat * to *, until 3 sts remain, slip 1, k2. Turn work.
Row 2: K2, p29, k2. Turn work.
Repeat Rows 1 and 2 until the heel flap is 30 rows. You are now at the beginning of right side.

TURN HEEL:
Row 1: K2, (slip 1, k1) 8 times, ssk, k1, turn work.
Row 2: Slip 1 purlwise, p4, p2tog, p1, turn work.
Row 3: Slip 1, *k1, slip 1*; repeat * to * until 1 st before the gap, ssk (1 st on both sides of the gap), k1, turn work.

➡

LEFT FOOT: Slip 1 knitwise, k8. Pick up Color B. Begin Row 1 on Chart B and knit the first 10 sts. Pick up and knit following the chart for 16 sts along the left side of the heel flap. Continue chart on Ndls 2 and 3. Pick up and knit following the chart for 16 sts along the right side of the heel flap. Knit the 9 remaining heel flap stitches onto Ndl 4. This is the new beginning of row.

Continue Chart B and work gusset decreases following the chart. At the top of Chart B, switch to Chart A and work the first 21 rows. Change to smaller needles and Color A, and begin toe. Toe is plain stockinette stitch. If the toe seems too large or your gauge changes, you can also work with two strands of Color A held together (take one yarn end from the outside and the other from the inside of the ball). K 1 row and begin toe decreases.

TOE DECREASES: At the end of Ndls 1 and 3, k2tog, k1. At the beginning of Ndls 2 and 4, k1, ssk. Work increases 4 times on every 2nd row and then on every row until 18 sts remain. K 1 row. Next row: Decrease as follows: at the end of Ndls 1 and 3, k3tog, k1. At the beginning of Ndls 2 and 4, k1, sssk. With 10 sts remaining, cut the yarn and pull through stitches.

Weave in ends and steam press the socks lightly. This pattern benefits especially from steaming, because the points where changes were made between needles can be quite uneven.

Row 4: Slip 1 purlwise, p until 1 st before the gap, p2tog (1 st on either side of the gap), p1, turn work. Repeat Rows 3 and 4 until all the side stitches have been decreased. You now have 19 sts on the needle and you are at the beginning of the right side.

RIGHT FOOT: Slip 1 knitwise, k9. Pick up Color B. Begin Row 1 on Chart B and knit the first 9 sts. Pick up and knit 16 sts along the left side of the heel flap following the chart. Continue chart on Ndls 2 and 3. Pick up and knit 16 sts along the right side of the heel flap following the chart. Knit the 10 remaining heel flap stitches onto Ndl 4. This is the new beginning of row.

B) RIGHT GUSSET

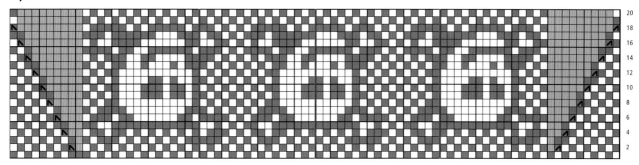

A) RIGHT LEG AND FOOT

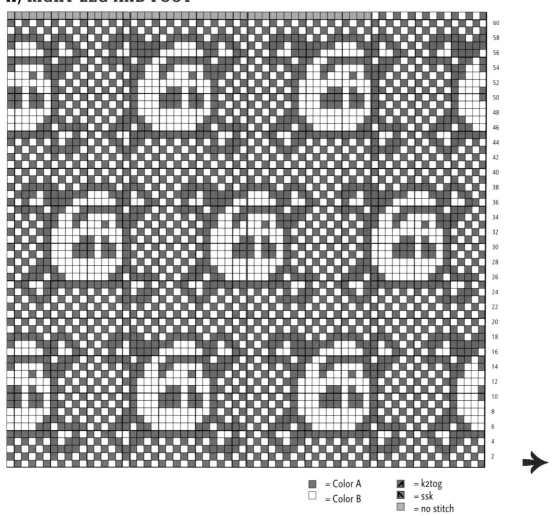

	= Color A		= k2tog
	= Color B		= ssk
			= no stitch

B) LEFT GUSSET

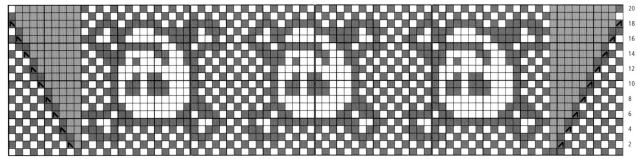

A) LEFT LEG AND FOOT

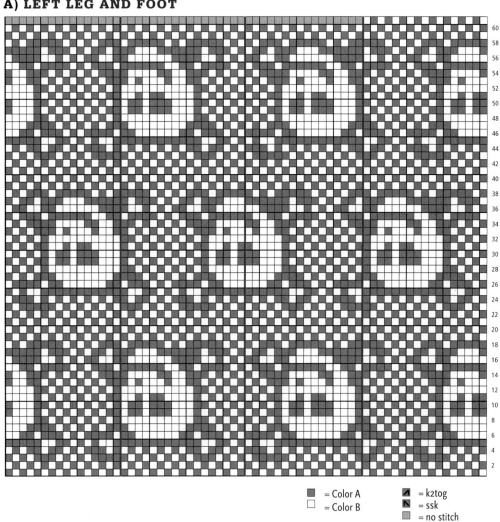

■ = Color A ◪ = k2tog
□ = Color B ◩ = ssk
▨ = no stitch

Chihuahua Mittens

These charming Chihuahua mittens incorporate a pretty picot edge and a simple gussetless thumb. The eyes are added at the end with duplicate stitching.

SKILL LEVEL: Experienced
SIZE: Large women's size
YARN: CYCA #3 (DK/light worsted)
Regia 6-ply
150 g / 375 m, 75% virgin wool /
25% polyamide
– Color A brown heather (02140), approx.
50 g
– Color B natural (01992), approx. 30 g
– Color C black (02066), a small amount
for eyes
NEEDLES: Set of double-pointed needles, U. S. size 1.5 / 2.5 mm for picot edge and size 2.5 / 3 mm for stranded knitting
GAUGE: 28 sts and 30 rows of stranded knitting = 4 x 4 in / 10 x 10 cm. Adjust needle size to obtain correct gauge if necessary.

PICOT EDGE: With Color A and smaller needles, cast on 60 sts (15 sts / needle). Join to work in the round. K 5 rows. Work the next round as follows: *k2tog, yo*; repeat * to * until the end of the row. K 5 rows. Fold the cuff at the yo row with wrong sides facing. Knit together the 1st stitch on your needles and the 1st stitch of your cast-on edge. Continue in the same manner until the end of the row.

Change to larger needles and begin stranded knitting following Chart A. **Note:** Each hand has its own chart. On Row 36 of the chart, place your thumb stitches onto scrap yarn. Here's how to do it: Knit 9 sts with a contrasting scrap yarn where indicated on

the chart. Return these stitches onto your left needle and continue the pattern with your working yarns. The scrap yarn is where your thumb will be.

With 12 sts remaining, cut the yarn and pull through stitches. Pull tight.

THUMB: Remove the scrap yarn and at the same time pick up the stitches from the bottom and top of the gap with smaller needles. Pick up an additional st from each end of the gap. You now have 20 stitches. Divide them onto 3 needles. K 20 rows or until your thumb is almost covered. On following rows, knit the first 2 sts together at the beginning of each needle. With 5 sts remaining, cut yarn, pull through the stitches and pull tight. If there are any holes at the start of the thumb, you can carefully sew them shut when weaving in ends.

Weave in ends before you start embroidering the dogs' faces.

THE EYES AND THE NOSE: Use black yarn and a needle. Make two horizontal stitches where indicated on Chart B (through both stitches), in each of the two eyes and in the nose, weaving in your yarn on the wrong side of the work. Be careful not to pull too tight. Weave in ends.

Steam press the mittens lightly.

B) EMBROIDERY RIGHT HAND

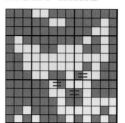

B) EMBROIDERY LEFT HAND

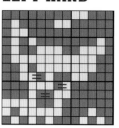

■ = Color A   ◪ = k2tog
□ = Color B   ◩ = ssk
                  ▨ = no stitch

A) RIGHT HAND

A) LEFT HAND

Chihuahua Socks

The Chihuahua Socks have a picot edge. The Dutch heel is made with stranded knitting. This pattern best fits a narrow foot, since there's no heel gusset. The eyes of the dogs are stitched onto the finished socks.

SKILL LEVEL: Experienced
SIZE: U. S. 7.5 / European 38
YARN: CYCA #3 (DK/light worsted) Regia 6-ply
150 g / 375 m, 75% virgin wool / 25% polyamide
– Color A brown heather (02140), approx. 65 g
– Color B natural (01992), approx. 50 g
– Color C black (02066), a small amount for eyes
NEEDLES: Set of double-pointed needles, U. S. size 1.5 / 2.5 mm for picot edge and 2.5 / 3 mm for stranded knitting
GAUGE: 28 sts and 30 rows of stranded knitting = 4 x 4 in / 10 x 10 cm. Adjust needle size to obtain correct gauge if necessary.

PICOT EDGE: With Color A and smaller needles, cast on 66 sts (16 sts / 17 sts / 16 sts / 17 sts) and join to work in the round. K 7 rows. Work the next round as follows: *k2tog, yo*; repeat * to * until the end of the row. K 7 rows. Fold the cuff at the yo row with wrong sides facing. Knit together the 1st stitch on your needles and the first 1st of your cast-on edge. Continue in the same manner until the end of the row. Change to larger needles and begin stranded knitting following Chart A.

At the top of Chart A, slip 2 sts from Ndl 3 to Ndl 2. Work the heel flap with the 33 sts remaining on Ndls 3 and 4. Turn work and begin Heel Chart. Make sure to twist the yarns on the wrong side before turning the work to avoid holes at the color changes.

At the top of the Heel Chart, you'll have 11 sts remaining after having just finished a right side row. With Color A, pick up and ktbl 11 sts along the left edge of the heel flap, catching Color B floats at appropriate places. Continue Chart B with the next 2 needles. With Color A, pick up and ktbl 11 sts along the right edge of the heel flap, catching Color B floats at appropriate places. Knit the remaining 9 heel flap sts onto this needle. This is the new beginning of row. Continue stranded knitting following Chart D. **Note:** This pattern does not have a heel gusset.

NOTE:

Each sock has its own chart! Only the Heel Chart is the same for both socks.

After finishing Row 48 of Chart D, work a decrease row with Color B as follows: k1 from Ndl 1 onto Ndl 4. You now have 3 needles in use. K2, ssk, k2tog, k2, sssk, k3, k3tog. With 11 sts remaining, cut yarn, pull through the stitches and pull tight. Weave in ends.

THE EYES AND THE NOSE: Use black yarn and a needle. Make two horizontal stitches where indicated on Chart B (through both stitches), in each of the two eyes and in the nose, weaving in your yarn on the wrong side of the work. Be careful not to pull too tight. Weave in the ends.

Steam press the socks lightly.

HEEL FLAP (same for both socks)

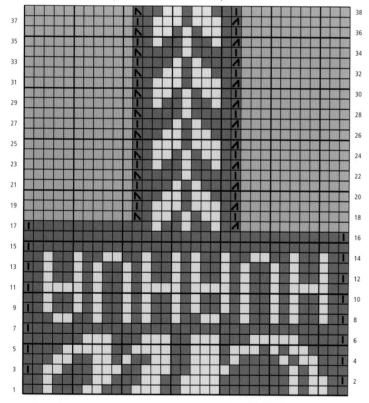

B) EMBROIDERY RIGHT FOOT

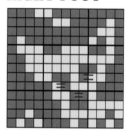

B) EMBROIDERY LEFT FOOT

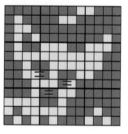

◥ = p2tog

◤ = ssk

▯ = slip kwise on right side, slip pwise on wrong side

▢ = no stitch

D) RIGHT FOOT

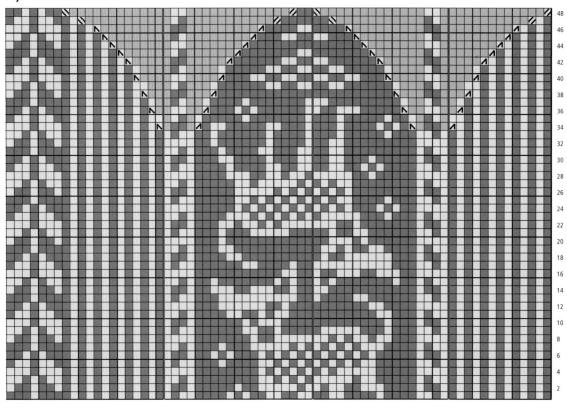

B) RIGHT FOOT

C) RIGHT FOOT

A) RIGHT LEG

D) LEFT FOOT

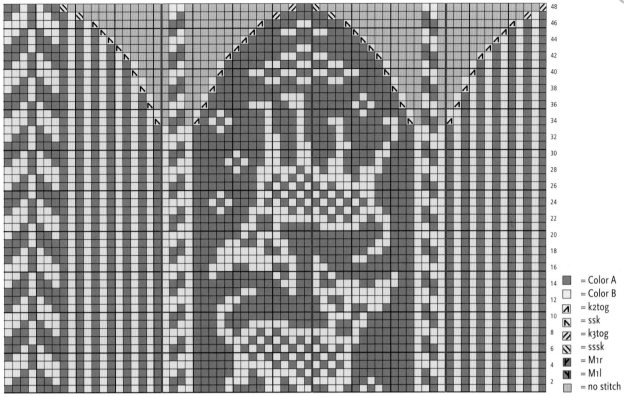

= Color A
= Color B
◢ = k2tog
◣ = ssk
◢ = k3tog
◣ = sssk
◤ = M1r
◥ = M1l
= no stitch

D) LEFT FOOT

A) LEFT FOOT

A) LEFT LEG

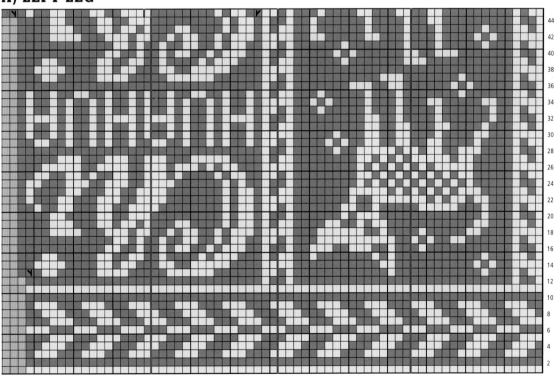

· ROSES ·

of the Mansion

Knit
WITH LOVE ·

· ROSE GARDEN ·

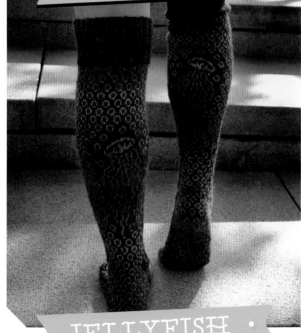

JELLYFISH ·

· KITTYCATS ·

Unruly Socks

STAFFIES

These Staffordshire-themed socks incorporate a reinforced Dutch heel. The eyes are added at the end with duplicate stitch.

SKILL LEVEL: Experienced
SIZE: U. S. 7.5 / European 38
YARN: CYCA #3 (DK/light worsted) Drops Karisma
50 g / 100 m, 100% wool
– Color A light gray (44), approx. 85 g
– Color B black (05), approx. 65 g
– Color C sea green (50), a small amount for eyes
NEEDLES: Set of double-pointed needles, U. S. size 4 / 3.5 mm for ribbing and 6 / 4 mm for stranded knitting
GAUGE: 22 sts and 24 rows of stranded knitting = 4 x 4 in / 10 x 10 cm. Adjust needle size to obtain correct gauge if necessary.

With Color A and smaller needles, cast on 52 sts (13 sts / needle). Join to work in the round. Work k2, p2 ribbing for 8 rows. Work one more row of ribbing and increase 2 sts. You now have 54 sts. K 3 rows. Change to larger needles and begin stranded knitting following Chart A. Divide onto needles as indicated by vertical lines. In this pattern, Color A should be the dominant color, so make sure you always cross it under the other color. At the top of Chart A, work the stitches on Ndls 1 and 2 following the chart. Leave Color B waiting; turn work and begin heel flap with Color A.

For heel flap, use the 26 sts on Ndls 1 and 2. P 1 row. Turn work.
Row 1 (RS): *Slip 1, k1*. Repeat * to * until the end of the row, turn work.
Row 2 (WS): Slip 1 purlwise, p25, turn work.
Repeat Rows 1 and 2 until the heel flap is 24 rows. You are now at the right side of work. Turn heel.

TURN HEEL:

Row 1: Repeat *slip 1, k1* until 10 sts remain, ssk, turn work.

Row 2: Slip 1 purlwise, p until 10 sts remain, p2tog, turn work.

Row 3: Slip 1, *k1, slip 1* until 1 st before the gap, ssk, turn work.

Row 4: Slip 1 purlwise, p until 1 st before the gap, p2tog, turn.

Repeat Rows 3 and 4 until all the side stitches have been decreased and you have 8 sts on the needle. Heel turn is now complete and you are on the right side of work.

With Color A, k4. You are now at the new beginning of row. Pick up Color B and begin stranded

knitting following Row 1 of Chart B. K 4, pick up and ktbl 14 sts along the left side of the heel flap following Chart B. Continue following the chart until the end of Ndl 3.

Pick up and ktbl 14 sts along the right side of the heel flap following Chart B. Continue Chart B and work gusset decreases following the chart. After completing Chart B, begin Chart C.

After toe decreases on Chart C, there are 10 sts remaining. Cut yarn, pull through the stitches, and pull tight. Weave in ends. Using Color C, work the eyes with duplicate stitch (see page 10). Weave in these ends also and steam press the socks lightly.

A) LEFT LEG

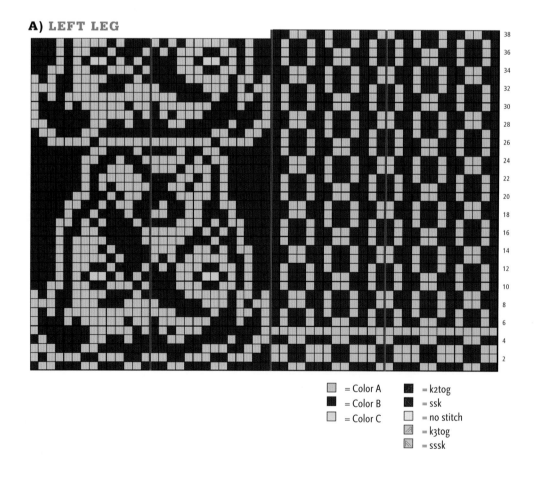

☐ = Color A	■ = k2tog
■ = Color B	▨ = ssk
☐ = Color C	☐ = no stitch
	◪ = k3tog
	◨ = sssk

C) LEFT FOOT

B) LEFT GUSSET

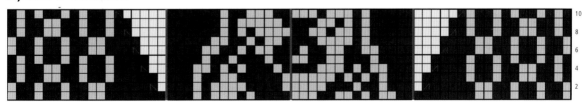

C) RIGHT FOOT

B) RIGHT GUSSET

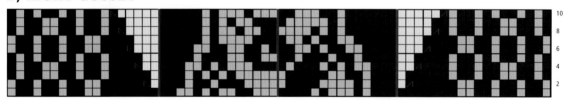

A) RIGHT LEG

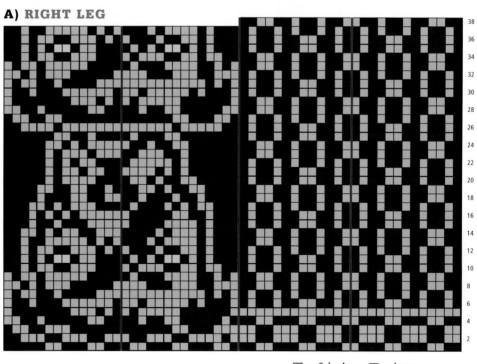

= Color A   = k2tog

= Color B   = ssk

= Color C   = no stitch

= k3tog

= sssk

NOTE:

Charts A, C, and F are the same for both socks. Charts B, D, and E are different for left and right socks.

ROSES OF THE MANSION •

The Roses of the Mansion pattern incorporates a double French heel and a double wedge toe. The gusset decreases are placed under the foot.

SKILL LEVEL: Experienced
SIZE: U. S. 7.5 / European 38
YARN: CYCA #1 (sock/finger-ling/baby) Regia 4-ply
50 g / 210 m, 75% wool / 25% polyamide
– Color A natural (01992), approx. 65 g
– Color B red heather (02742), approx. 55 g
NEEDLES: Set of double-pointed needles, U. S. size 2.5 / 3 mm for stranded knitting, 1.5 and 0 / 2.5 mm and 2 mm for heel and toe
GAUGE: 32 sts and 33 rows of stranded knitting = 4 x 4 in / 10 x 10 cm. Adjust needle size to obtain correct gauge if necessary.

Before you begin knitting, cut a strand of 25 inches from Color A. You will use this later for the heel.

With Color A and needles U. S. size 1.5 / 2.5 mm, cast on 70 sts (17 sts / 18 sts / 17 sts / 18 sts) and join to work in the round. Follow Chart A for cuff lace (chart repeats 10 times per row). After completing Chart A, k 9 rows, p 1 row, k 14 rows. Turn the cuff inside out and change to U. S. size 2.5 / 3 mm needles. Divide the stitches onto needles as indicated by vertical lines in Chart B, and begin stranded knitting. Complete Chart B and begin heel flap.

The heel is double and both layers are knitted separately back and forth with stitches on Ndls 1 and 2 (35 sts). With Colors A and B held together, knit the stitches on Ndls 1 and 2 onto a needle U. S. size 1.5 / 2.5 mm. Next, separate Color A stitches onto a needle on the wrong side of work and Color B stitches onto a needle on the right side of work (35 sts on both needles). Slip the Color A stitches onto scrap yarn and use Color A to work heel, starting with the Color B stitches.

COLOR A HEEL (needles size 1.5): Turn work. You are at the start of a wrong side row. With Color A, p35, turn work. Slip 1 knitwise, k34. Turn work. Slip 1 purlwise, p34. Turn work and begin Lace Chart C. Complete Chart C and begin heel turn.

A) CUFF LACE

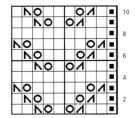

☐ = knit
■ = purl
◢ = k2tog
◣ = ssk
○ = yarn over

E) LEFT FOOT

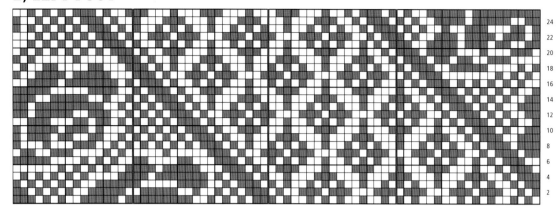

D) LEFT GUSSET

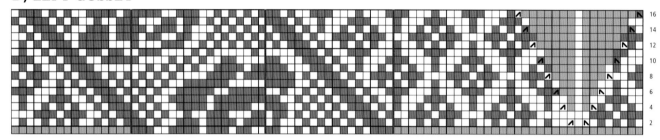

E) LEFT LEG

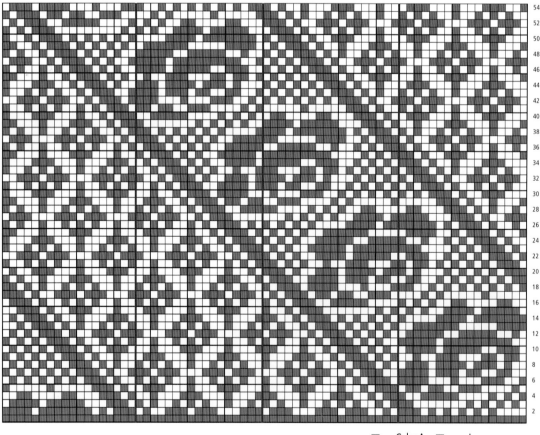

☐ = Color A   ◨ = ssk

■ = Color B   ◪ = k2tog

▨ = no stitch

TURN HEEL:

Row 1 (RS): Slip 1 knitwise, k until 16 sts remain, ssk, k1 turn work.

Row 2 (WS): Slip 1 purlwise, p until 16 sts remain, p2tog, p 1, turn work.

Row 3: Slip 1 knitwise, k until 1 st before the gap, ssk (1 st on both sides of the gap), k1, turn.

Row 4: Slip 1 purlwise, p until 1 st before the gap, p2tog (1 st on both sides of the gap), p1, turn. Repeat Rows 3 and 4 until all the side stitches have been decreased. (On the last two rows, there is no stitch after ssk or p2tog.) You now have 19 sts on the needle and you have just completed a wrong side row. Leave this side of heel waiting and begin the other heel layer with Color B.

COLOR B HEEL (needles U. S. size 0 / 2 mm): Pick up the stitches on the scrap yarn. Turn work. You are at the start of a wrong side row. With Color B, p35, turn work. Work 30 rows stockinette stitch in total (including the first Color A row); slip the 1st st knitwise on right side rows and slip the 1st st purlwise on wrong side rows. Turn heel.

TURN HEEL:

Row 1 (RS): Slip 1 knitwise, k until 16 sts remain, ssk, k1, turn work.

Row 2 (WS): Slip 1 purlwise, p until 16 sts remain, p2tog, p 1, turn work.

Row 3: Slip 1 knitwise, k until 1 st before the gap, ssk (1 st on both sides of the gap), k1, turn.

Row 4: Slip 1 purlwise, p until 1 st before the gap, p2tog (1 st on both sides of the gap), p1, turn. Repeat Rows 3 and 4 until all the side stitches have been decreased. (On the last two rows there is no stitch after ssk or p2tog.) You now have 19 sts on the needle and you have just completed a wrong side row.

Place the two needles side by side. Ndl 1 has 19 Color B stitches and Ndl 2 has 19 Color A stitches. Drop Color A. With Color B, knit together the 1st st on Ndl 1 and the 1st st on Ndl 2. Continue in this manner until the end of the row. You now have 19 Color B sts and the two heel layers have been attached to each other. With Color B, pick up and knit 16 sts along the left side of the heel flap, pulling the yarn through both heel layers to attach them (35 sts on the needle). Now you need the Color A strand you cut at the beginning. Use it to work Row 1 of Chart D across Ndls 2 and 3.

Drop the Color A yarn and with Color B, pick up and knit 16 sts along the right side of the heel flap, pulling the yarn through both heel layers to attach them.

A) HEEL LACE

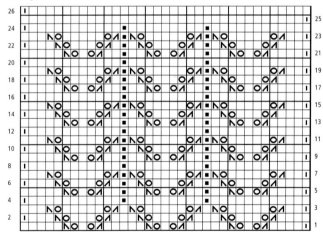

☐ = k on RS, p on WS

▪ = p on RS, k on WS

◪ = k2tog on RS, ssp (slip 2 sts knitwise one by one on the right needle, return them to the left needle and p2tog) on WS

◩ = ssk on RS, p2togtbl on WS

◉ = yarn over

Ⅰ = slip 1 knitwise on RS, slip 1 purlwise on WS

You are now at the beginning of the row. Pick up the strand of Color A you left waiting and continue Chart D on needles U. S. size 2.5 / 3 mm. Work gusset decreases as indicated on Chart D. The gusset decreases are placed under the foot. After Chart D, begin Chart E. After completing Chart E, begin toe.

The toe is double and both layers are knitted separately in the round. With Color A and B held together, k 1 row. Next, separate Color A stitches onto their own needles. Color B stitches are on the outer needles and Color A stitches on the inner needles (70 sts of both colors). Slip the Color B stitches onto scrap yarn and use Color B to work the toe, starting with the Color A stitches.

COLOR B TOE: Leave the Color A yarn waiting on the right side of work. Change to needles U. S. size 0 / 2 mm and, with Color B, k 2 rows. Place the

stitches onto needles as follows: 19 sts / 17 sts / 18 sts / 16 sts. Begin Chart F, but instead of lace, knit the whole toe in stockinette stitch. Before the last toe decrease, slip 1 st from Ndl 1 to Ndl 4. With 11 sts remaining, cut yarn, pull through the stitches, and pull tight. Move to Color A toe.

COLOR A TOE: Pick up the stitches on scrap yarn with needles U. S. size 1.5 / 2.5 mm. Divide the stitches onto needles as follows: 19 sts / 17 sts / 18 sts / 16 sts. With Color A, k 2 rows. Begin lace, following Chart F. Before the last toe decrease, slip 1 st from Ndl 1 to Ndl 4. With 11 sts remaining, pull through the stitches, and pull tight.

Weave in ends and steam press the socks lightly.

A) TOE

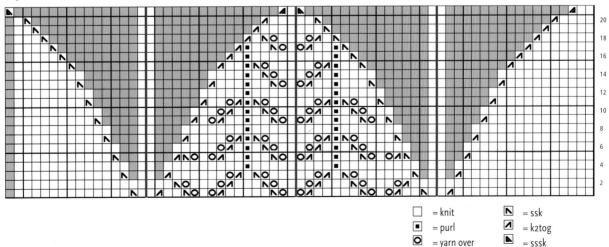

☐	= knit	◣	= ssk
▪	= purl	◢	= k2tog
◉	= yarn over	◥	= sssk
▨	= no stitch	◪	= k3tog

E) RIGHT FOOT

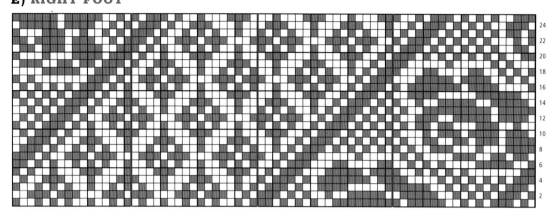

D) RIGHT GUSSET

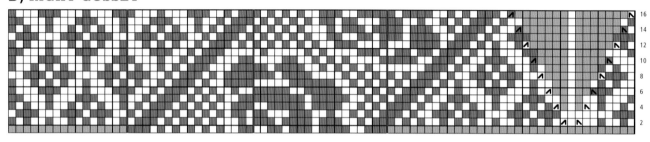

B) RIGHT LEG

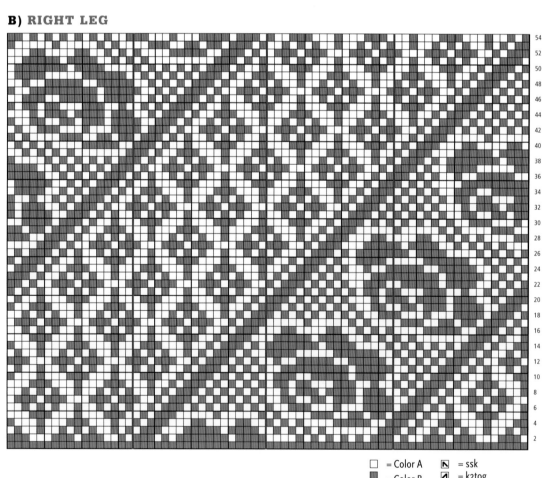

□ = Color A   ◣ = ssk
■ = Color B   ◢ = k2tog
▨ = no stitch

·KNIT WITH LOVE·

Knit with Love socks incorporate a well-fitting "Grand-mother Alma" heel, knitted with stitches on one needle. There's no heel turn. The cuff has a few rows with three colors, but the rest of the sock is regular two-color stranded knitting.

SKILL LEVEL: Experienced
SIZE: U. S. 6.5 / European 37
YARN: CYCA #3 (DK/light worsted) Regia 6-ply
150 g / 375 m, 75% virgin wool / 25% polyamide
– Color A dark gray (06047), approx. 70 g
– Color B white (06860), approx. 15 g
– Color C anthracite heather (00522), approx. 5 g
– Color D pink (06345), approx. 10 g
NEEDLES: Set of double-pointed needles, U. S. size 1.5 / 2.5 mm
GAUGE: 30 sts and 32 rows of stranded knitting = 4 x 4 in / 10 x 10 cm. Adjust needle size to obtain correct gauge if necessary.

With Color A, cast on 70 sts (17 sts / 18 sts / 17 sts / 18 sts) and join to work in the round. K 1 row. Work k1, p1 ribbing for 10 rows. K 2 rows and p 1 row. Continue to Chart A to start the heart pattern. The pattern repeats 7 times per row.

After completing Chart A, work 1 row of p2, k2 ribbing with Color A, beginning the row with p2. K2tog twice during this row to decrease 2 sts. You now have 68 sts.
Next row: Knit.
Next row: P2, k2 across.
Repeat these two rows for about 2 inches. The last row should be a p2, k2 row. Begin heel.

HEEL: K 18. The heel flap is knitted back and forth across these stitches. Leave the other stitches on hold.
Row 1: Turn work, *k2, p2*; repeat * to * until 2 sts remain, k2.
Row 2: Turn work, k18.
Repeat these two rows until the heel flap is 34 rows. You have now completed the heel and finished knitting a right side row.

Pick up and knit 17 sts along the left side of the heel flap. Knit across to the right edge of the heel flap. Pick up and knit 17 sts along the right side of the heel flap. Knit the 9 heel stitches onto Ndl 4. This is the new beginning of row.

Begin stranded knitting following Chart B and work
the gusset decreases as indicated. You might want to
add a 6th needle at this point, if possible. Arrange the
stitches across the needles as best suits you, as long
as you make note of the start of the row and continue
following the chart. You have 68 sts after the gusset
decreases.

After completing Chart B, work 1 row of p2, k2 ribbing
and k2tog once on every needle. You now have 64 sts.
Next row: Knit.
Next row: P2, k2 across.
Repeat these two rows for about 1½ in / 3 cm. The last
row should be a p2, k2 row.
Next row: (K2tog, k2) across.
You now have 48 sts. Work 1 row p1, k2 ribbing. K 1
row. Begin toe decreases. The rest of the sock is stock-
inette stitch.

TOE DECREASES: Make sure you have 12 sts
on each needle. At the end of Ndls 1 and 3, k2tog, k1.
At the beginning of Ndls 2 and 4, k1, ssk. Repeat these
decreases 2 times every other row, and then every
row until you have 8 sts remaining. Cut yarn and pull
through stitches. Weave in ends on the wrong side of
work. Steam press the socks lightly.

= Color A
= Color B
= Color C
= Color D

= k2tog
= ssk
= no stitch

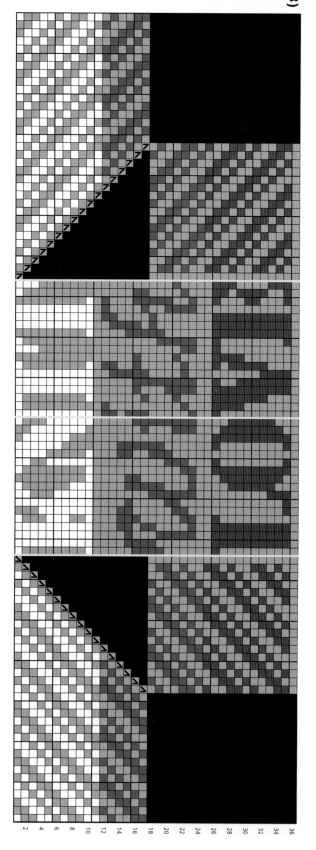

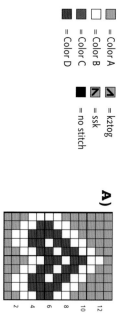

A)

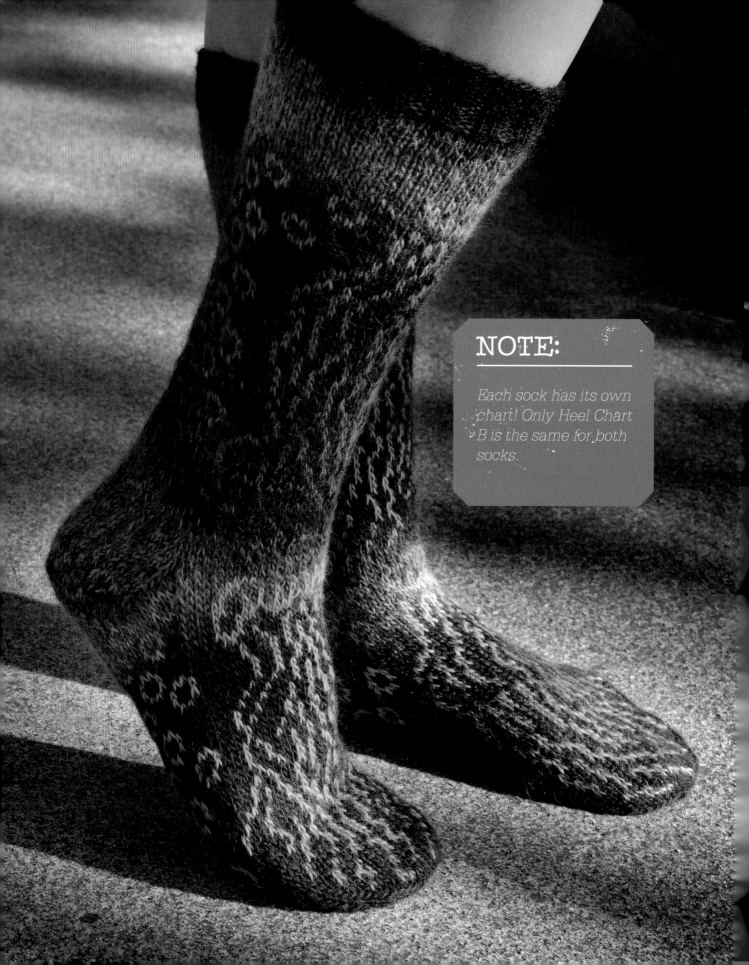

NOTE:

Each sock has its own chart! Only Heel Chart B is the same for both socks.

JELLYFISH •

*You can choose whether to knit short leg or over-the-knee leg.
The over-the-knee leg has some shaping. The socks incorporate
a stranded French heel and a wedge toe. Use Kitchener stitch to
close the toe.*

SKILL LEVEL: Experienced
SIZE: 7.5 / European 38
YARN: CYCA #2 (sport/baby)
Drops Delight
50 g / 175 m, 75% wool /
25% polyamide
– Color A turquoise / purple
(09), approx. 80 g (if you want
matching socks, you should
have three balls of yarn)
CYCA #1 (sock/fingering/baby)
Lang Yarns Jawoll Magic
100 g / 400m, 75% wool /
25% polyamide
– Color B pink (84.0019),
approx. 40 g
NEEDLES: Set of dou-
ble-pointed needles, U. S. size
1.5 / 2.5 mm for ribbing and 2.5
/ 3 mm for stranded knitting
GAUGE: 32 sts and 33 rows
of stranded knitting = 4 x 4 in /
10 x 10 cm. Adjust needle
size to obtain correct gauge if
necessary.

With Color A and smaller needles, cast on 68 sts (17 sts / needle) and join to work in the round. Work k2, p2 ribbing for 12 rows. Work 1 more ribbing row, increasing 3 stitches evenly spaced along the row. You now have 71 sts. K 2 rows. Change to larger needles and begin stranded knitting following Chart A.

After completing Chart A, begin the heel. Follow Chart B to knit the heel flap back and forth across the stitches on Ndls 1 and 2. Make sure to twist the yarns on the wrong side before turning the work to avoid making holes on the heel.

After completing Chart B, you have 25 sts on the needle. Cut Color A and put the first 12 sts on hold. The new beginning of row is after these stitches. Pick up another strand of Color A and begin Row 1 of Chart C. Work the first 11 sts, ssk, and continue following Chart C as you pick up and ktbl 12 sts along the left edge of the heel flap. Knit the stitches on Ndls 2 and 3. Continue following Chart C as you pick up and ktbl 12 sts along the right side of the heel flap. Work the last 12 sts that were put on hold earlier. You have completed Row 1 of Chart C. Continue following Chart C.

After completing Chart C, you have 18 sts remaining and have just finished Ndl 1. Cut the yarn, leaving a tail approx. 10 in / 20 cm long, and use Color A and Kitchener stitch to close the toe.

KITCHENER STITCH TOE: Slip stitches from Ndl 4 onto Ndl 1 and from Ndl 3 onto Ndl 2. You now have 2 needles in use. Place the needles facing each other and turn work so that the jellyfish are facing you. Pick up a third needle.

1. Purl the 1st st on the front needle; drop it off the needle and pull yarn through.
Knit the 2nd st on the front needle; pull yarn through and leave the stitch on the needle.
2. Knit the 1st st on the back needle; drop it off the needle and pull yarn through.

Purl the 2nd st on the back needle; pull yarn through and leave the stitch on the needle.
Repeat 1 and 2 until 2 sts remain.
Purl the 1st st on the front needle; drop it off the needle and pull yarn through.
Knit the 1st st on the back needle; drop it off the needle and pull yarn through.

Weave in ends and steam press the socks lightly.

B) HEEL (same for both socks)

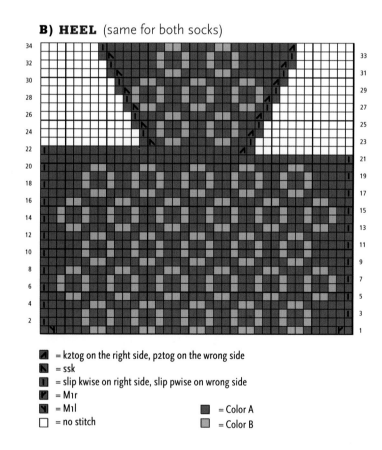

= k2tog on the right side, p2tog on the wrong side

= ssk

= slip kwise on right side, slip pwise on wrong side

= M1r

= M1l

= no stitch

= Color A

= Color B

□ = Color A
◥ = Color B
◪ = ssk
◩ = k2tog
▨ = no stitch

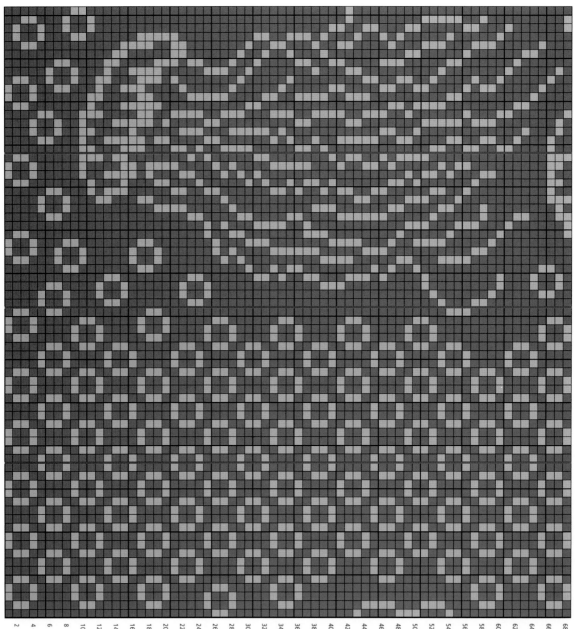

2 4 6 8 10 12 14 16 18 20 22 24 26 28 30 32 34 36 38 40 42 44 46 48 50 52 54 56 58 60 62 64 66 68

A) LEFT LEG

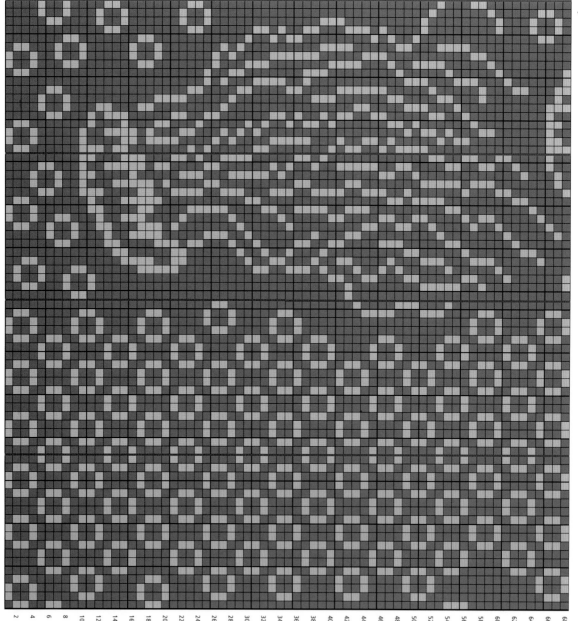

2 4 6 8 10 12 14 16 18 20 22 24 26 28 30 32 34 36 38 40 42 44 46 48 50 52 54 56 58 60 62 64 66 68

C) LEFT FOOT

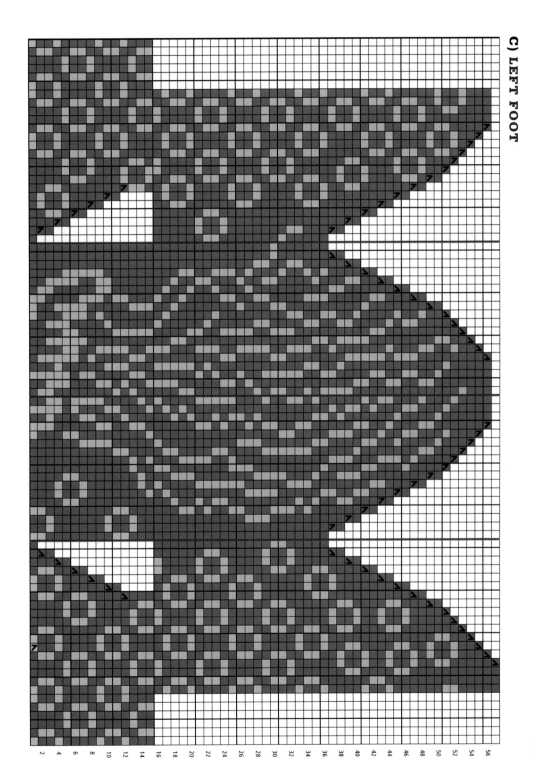

2 4 6 8 10 12 14 16 18 20 22 24 26 28 30 32 34 36 38 40 42 44 46 48 50 52 54 56

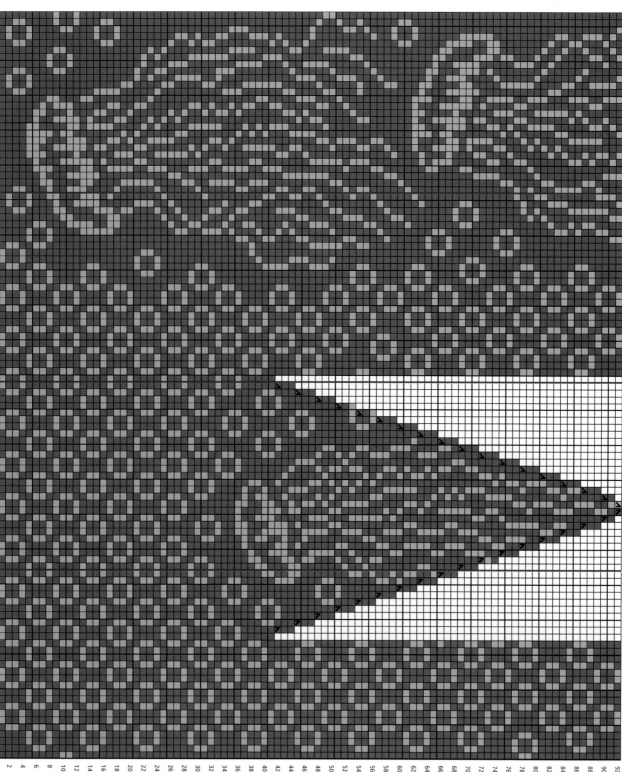

= Color A
= Color B
= ssk
= k2tog
= no stitch

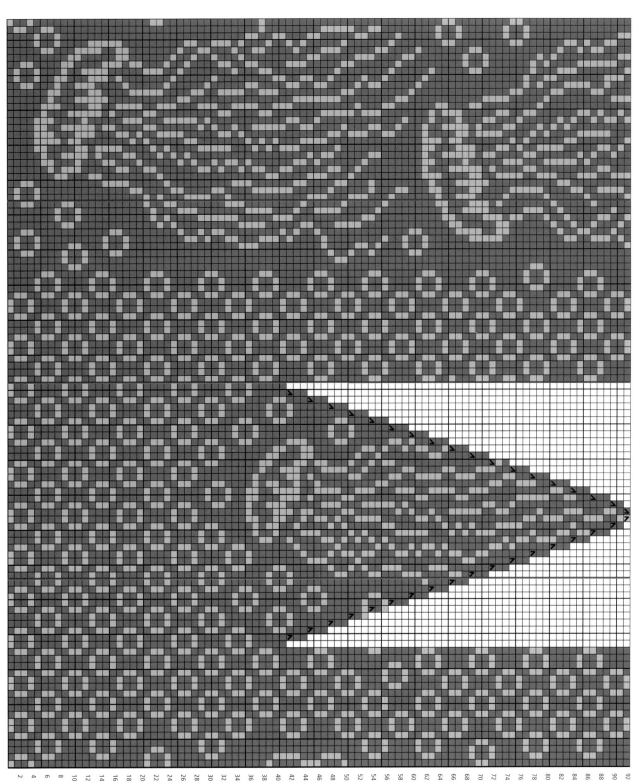

NOTE:

Each sock has its own chart! Only Heel Chart B is the same for both socks.

Over-the-Knee
·JELLYFISH·

With Color A and smaller needles, cast on 108 sts (27 sts / needle) and join to work in the round. Work k2, p2 ribbing for 3 inches. On the last ribbing row, k2tog to decrease 1 stitch. You now have 107 sts. K 2 rows. Change to larger needles and begin stranded knitting following Chart D.

After completing Chart D, you have 71 sts remaining. Continue with Row 41 of Chart A, arranging your stitches on the needles as indicated by vertical lines. From this point on, follow the Jellyfish pattern.

SKILL LEVEL: Experienced

SIZE: U. S. 7.5 / European 38; circumference at the calf approx. 14 in / 35 cm, length of leg from under the heel approx. 23 in / 59 cm

YARN: CYCA #1 (sock/fingering/baby) Lang Yarns Mille Colori Socks & Lace Luxe
100 g / 400 m, 73 % wool / 23% polyamide / 2% polyester
– Color A blue (859 0035), approx. 130 g
CYCA #1 (sock/fingering/baby) Lang Yarns Jawoll Magic
100 g / 400 m, 75% wool / 25% polyamide
– Color B pink (84.0019), approx. 55 g

NEEDLES: Set of double-pointed needles, U. S. size 1.5 / 2.5 mm for ribbing and 2.5 / 3 mm for stranded knitting

GAUGE: 32 sts and 33 rows of stranded knitting = 4 x 4 in / 10 x 10 cm. Adjust needle size to obtain correct gauge if necessary.

ROSE GARDEN

The picot edge is created with the knitted cast on. The easy mock cables continue all the way down to the heel turn. The sock has a round toe.

SKILL LEVEL: Experienced
SIZE: U. S. 7.5 / European 38
YARN: CYCA #1 (sock/fingering/baby) Regia 4-ply
50 g / 210 m, 75% wool / 25% polyamide
– Color A leaf green (02744), approx. 70 g
– Color B natural (01992), approx. 15 g
NEEDLES: Set of double-pointed needles, U. S. size 1.5 / 2.5 mm
GAUGE: 28 sts and 40 rows = 4 x 4 in / 10 x 10 cm of stockinette stitch. Adjust needle size to obtain correct gauge if necessary.

GARDEN BOBBLE: Cast on 3 sts with knitted cast on (see page 10), k2, pull the right stitch over the left stitch, k1, pull the right stitch over the left stitch.

With Color A, make a slip knot. Make 11 garden bobbles. *Use knitted cast on to make 1 st, make 11 garden bobbles.* Repeat * to * until you have 60 sts. Divide the stitches onto 4 needles (15 sts / needle). Turn work inside out and join to work in the round. Begin lace following Chart A. The pattern repeats 5 times per row.

After finishing Chart A, k 2 rows with Color A. Knit one more row, increasing 1 st on each needle. You now have 64 sts. Begin stranded knitting following Chart B.

After finishing Chart B, k 2 rows with Color A. Knit one more row and increase 1 st on Ndl 1. You now have 65 sts.

Begin mock cables following Chart C. The cable pattern repeats 13 times per row. Repeat Rows 1–4 of Chart C 7 times total, or until leg is desired length. Knit Rows 1 and 2 of Chart C. Begin heel.

Work the heel back and forth across the 33 sts on Ndls 1 and 2. Begin Chart D.

At the end of Chart D you have 32 heel sts. Knit 1 row around the sock as follows: K 11 double sts (= slip each st purlwise and pull the yarn so tight that the stitch turns around and it looks like you have two sts on the needle), continue the mock cable pattern on the next 2 needles, k 11 double sts.

The rest of the heel is stockinette stitch knitted back and forth. K11, turn work. Make a double stitch, p11, turn work. *Make a double stitch, k until you reach the double stitch made on the previous row, k the double stitch, k1, turn work. Make a double stitch, p until you reach the double stitch made on the previous row, p the double stitch, p1, turn work.* Repeat * to * until you can make one last double stitch at the beginning of a right side row. Make the double stitch, k15. This is the new beginning of row. The heel is complete and you now have 64 sts. The rest of the sock is worked in the round.

Knit stockinette stitch on Ndls 1 and 4 and continue mock cables on Ndls 2 and 3. When the length of the foot is about 6½ in and you have finished Row 3 of Chart C, k 1 row and work yo following the chart. K 2 rows. Work Rows 1–5 of Chart B. Begin toe decreases.

TOE DECREASES:
K 2 rows.
1st decrease row: *K4, k2tog*. Repeat * to * until 4 sts remain, k2, k2tog.
K 4 rows.
2nd decrease row: *K3, k2tog*. Repeat * to * until 3 sts remain, k3.
K 3 rows.
3rd decrease row: *K2, k2tog*. Repeat * to * until 3 sts remain, k1, k2tog.
K 2 rows.
4th decrease row: *K1, k2tog*. Repeat * to * until the end of the row.
K 1 row.
5th decrease row: *K2tog* Repeat * to * until 1 st remains, k1.
6th decrease row: *K2tog* Repeat * to * until 1 st remains, k1.

You have 6 sts remaining. Cut the yarn, pull through the stitches, and pull tight. Weave in ends and steam press the socks lightly.

A) CUFF LACE

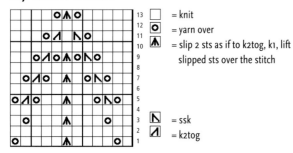

= knit
= yarn over
= slip 2 sts as if to k2tog, k1, lift slipped sts over the stitch

= ssk
= k2tog

C) MOCK CABLE

= knit
= purl
= yarn over
= slip 1 st as if to knit, k2, lift slipped st over these 2 sts

D) HEEL

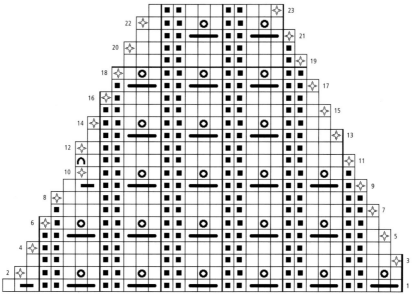

☐ = k on right side, p on wrong side

■ = p on right side, k on wrong side

▬ = slip 1 st as if to knit, k2, lift slipped st over these 2 sts

▬ = slip 1 st as if to knit, k1, lift slipped st over the stitch

O = yarn over

✧ = lift yarn on the needle as if to start purling
and pull tight to form a double stitch on the needle

∩ = lift the bar between stitches onto the needle and knit

B)

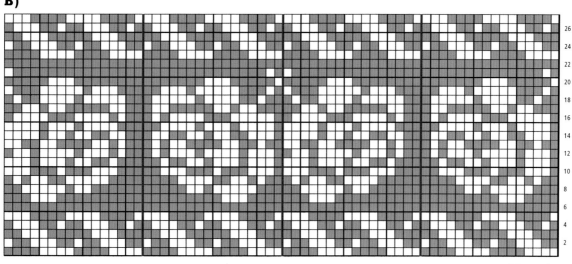

▨ = Color A
☐ = Color B

Spooky
CHRISTMAS SOCKS •

These Christmas-themed socks are a bit on the unconventional side! They incorporate a reinforced Dutch heel and a reinforced toe. There are some decreases at the ankle.

SKILL LEVEL: Experienced
SIZE: U. S. 7.5 / European 38; length of leg from under the heel approx. 16 in / 41 cm, circumference at the calf approx. 14¼ in / 36 cm
YARN: CYCA #3 (DK/light worsted) Drops Karisma 50 g / 100 m, 100% wool
– Color A red (18), approx. 65 g
– Color B navy blue (17), approx. 60 g
– Color C white (19), approx. 50 g
– Color D bright blue (07), approx. 35 g
– Color E lemon (79), a small amount for the lantern
– Color F forest green (47), approx. 5 g
NEEDLES: Set of double-pointed needles, U. S. size 4 / 3.5 mm for ribbing and 6 / 4 mm for stranded knitting
GAUGE: 22 sts and 24 rows of stranded knitting = 4 x 4 in / 10 x 10 cm. Adjust needle size to obtain correct gauge if necessary.

With Color A and smaller needles, cast on 64 sts (16 sts / needle) and join to work in the round. Work k2, p2 ribbing for 9 rows. Increase 2 sts on the last ribbing row. You now have 66 sts. With Color B, k 1 row; with Color A, k 1 row. Change to larger needles and begin stranded knitting following Chart A. **Note:** Each sock has its own leg chart; the rest of the charts are the same for both socks. After completing Chart A, divide the stitches onto needles as indicated by the vertical lines in Chart B. At the end of Chart B, you have 54 sts remaining. Begin heel.

HEEL FLAP: With Color A, knit the stitches on Ndl 1 onto Ndl 4. You now have 27 sts for the heel. Turn work.
Row 1 (WS): Slip 1 purlwise, p26, turn work.
Row 2 (RS): *Slip 1, k1*; repeat * to * until 1 st remains, k1, turn work.
Repeat Rows 1 and 2 until the heel flap is 24 rows and you have just finished a right side row.
Turn work and begin turning the heel.

TURN HEEL:
Row 1: Slip 1 purlwise, p until 10 sts remain, p2tog, turn work.
Row 2: Slip 1 knitwise, repeat *k1, slip 1* until 10 sts remain, ssk, turn work.
Row 3: Slip 1 purlwise, p until 1 st before the gap, p2tog, turn work.
Row 4: Slip 1, *k1, slip 1* until 1 st before the gap, ssk, turn work.

Repeat Rows 3 and 4 until all the side stitches have been decreased and you have 9 sts on the needle. Heel turn is now complete and you have just finished knitting a right side row.

Slip the 1st 5 heel flap sts onto another needle and keep on hold. You are now at the new beginning of row. Change into Color B, k4. Pick up and ktbl 14 sts along the left side of the heel flap onto Ndl 1. Knit the stitches on Ndls 2 and 3. Pick up and ktbl 14 sts along the right side of the heel flap onto Ndl 4, and then knit the 5 sts on hold onto the same needle.

Make sure the stitches are divided across the needles as indicated in Chart C and begin stranded knitting. Follow the chart for gusset decreases. After the decreases you have 56 sts remaining. Divide them across the needles as indicated in Chart D and begin Chart D.

After toe decreases, there are 10 sts remaining. Cut yarn, pull through the stitches and pull tight. Weave in ends. Using Color E, work the lanterns with duplicate stitch (see page 10). Weave in these ends also and steam press the socks lightly.

A) RIGHT LEG

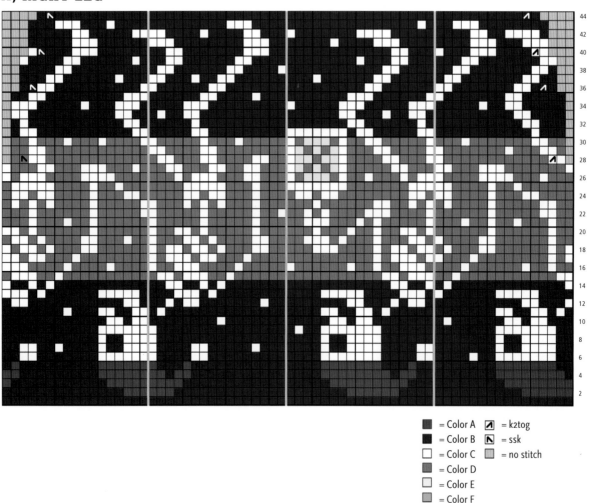

■ = Color A	◸ = k2tog
■ = Color B	◹ = ssk
□ = Color C	▨ = no stitch
▦ = Color D	
▫ = Color E	
▪ = Color F	

A) LEFT LEG

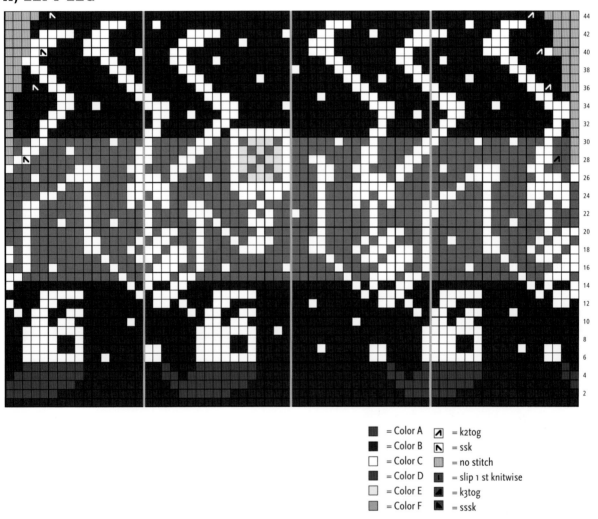

	= Color A		= k2tog
= Color B		= ssk
= Color C		= no stitch
= Color D		= slip 1 st knitwise
= Color E		= k3tog
= Color F		= sssk

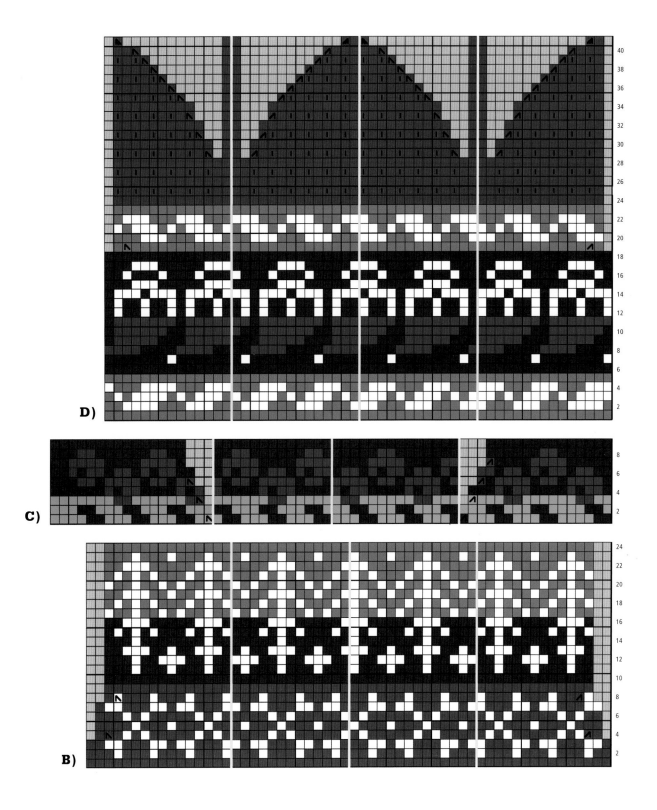

D)

C)

B)

· KITTYCATS ·

The Kittycats pattern incorporates a reinforced French heel and a reinforced toe. As a decoration, you can weave a twisted cord through the eyelets, make cute pompoms with a fork, and attach them on the ends.

SKILL LEVEL: Experienced
SIZE: U. S. 7.5–8.5 / European 38–39
YARN: CYCA #2 (sport/baby) Drops Fabel
50 g / 205 m, 75% wool / 25% polyamide
– Color A gray (200), approx. 75 g
– Color B off-white (100), approx. 35 g
NEEDLES: Set of double-pointed needles, U. S. sizes 1.5 and 2.5 / 2.5 and 3 mm
GAUGE: 32 sts and 33 rows of stranded knitting = 4 x 4 in / 10 x 10 cm. Adjust needle size to obtain correct gauge if necessary.

With Color A and smaller needles, cast on 72 sts (18 sts / needle) and join to work in the round. Work k2, p2 ribbing for 10 rows. K 1 row and begin Chart A; the pattern repeats 12 times per row. At the end of Chart A, knit 1 row and increase 1 st at the end of Ndl 4. You now have 73 sts. Change to larger needles and begin Chart B. **Note:** Each leg has its own chart. At the top of Chart B, change to smaller needles. With Color A, k 1 row and decrease 1 st at the end of Ndl 4. You now have 72 sts. Work Chart A; the pattern repeats 12 times per row. At the end of Chart A, k 1 row with Color A, cut yarns and begin heel.

HEEL FLAP: For heel, use the 36 sts on Ndls 4 and 1. Turn work. Pick up a new strand of Color A. You will begin the heel with a wrong side row beginning at the end of Ndl 1.
Row 1 (WS): Slip 1 purlwise, p35, turn work.
Row 2 (RS): *Slip 1, k1*. Repeat * to * until the end of the row. Turn work.
Repeat Rows 1 and 2 until the heel flap is 36 rows and you have just finished a right side row.

TURN HEEL:
Row 1: Slip 1 purlwise, p20, p2tog, p1, turn work.
Row 2: Slip 1 knitwise, k7, ssk, k1, turn work.

NOTE:

Chart B has a right and a left leg version. All the other charts are the same for both socks.

Row 3: Slip 1 purlwise, p until 1 st before the gap, p2tog (1 st on both sides of the gap), p1, turn work.
Row 4: Slip 1 knitwise, k until 1 st before the gap, ssk (1 st on both sides of the gap), k1, turn work. Repeat Rows 3 and 4 until all the side stitches have been decreased. You now have 22 sts on the needle and you have completed a right side row. The heel turn is now complete.

With Color A, pick up and ktbl 18 sts along the left edge of the heel. Knit across Ndls 2 and 3. Pick up and ktbl 18 sts along the right side of the heel flap onto Ndl 4. Knit additional 11 heel flap sts onto Ndl 4. You are now at the new beginning of row.

Change to larger needles and begin stranded knitting and gusset decreases following Chart C. After completing Chart C, begin Chart D; the pattern repeats 12 times per row. After completing Chart D, change to smaller needles and knit 1 row with Color A. Work Chart A one more time—remember, the pattern repeats 12 times per row—and then begin Chart E.

At the end of Chart E, you have 8 sts remaining. Cut the yarn and pull through stitches. Pull tight and weave in all the ends on the wrong side of work. Steam press the socks lightly.

CORD: Cut a length of about 140 in / 360 cm of your yarn and fold it in half. Hold one end of the yarn and ask a friend to hold the other end (you can also loop the yarn around an object, as long as you can lift the cord off it in the end). Step back until the yarn is straight but not tight. Keeping the yarns together, twist them in the same direction until the cord seems pretty tight. Fold it carefully in half and let it twist on itself. If there are any uneven spots, smooth them out by pulling gently with your fingers. Tie a knot at the open end. Weave the cord through the knitted eyelets so the ends come out at the back of the sock.

POMPOM: Use a fork to make a pompom. Cut a 10-inch strand of yarn and let it hang between the middle tines of the fork. Wrap the yarn from your yarn ball about 70 times around the fork tines. With the separate length of yarn, make a simple knot around the wraps and pull the bundle off the fork. Tighten the knot and make another one. Cut the loops. Do not cut the ends of the middle yarn yet; use them to attach the pompom to the end of the cord, and then fluff the pompom and trim as needed.

A)

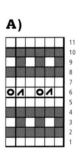

⊿ = k2tog

◎ = yarn over

■ = Color A

□ = Color B

D)

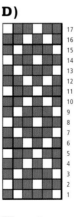

■ = Color A

□ = Color B

B) RIGHT LEG

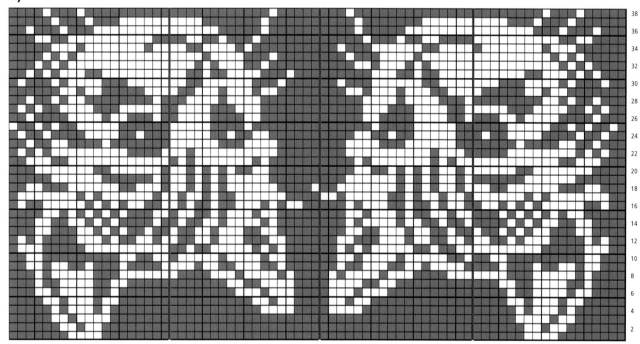

B) LEFT LEG

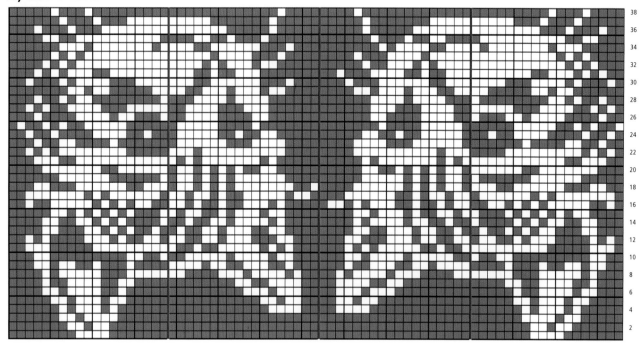

■ = Color A
□ = Color B

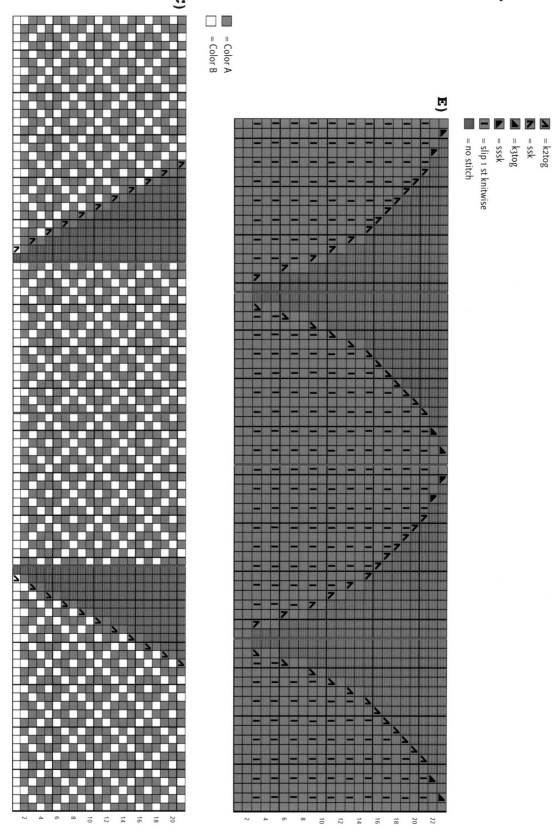

C)

■ = Color A
□ = Color B

E)

■ = k2tog
◣ = ssk
▬ = k3tog
◥ = sssk
— = slip 1 st knitwise
□ = no stitch

· LUPINES ·

The Lupines design incorporates a short-row heel and a wedge toe. The stems are crocheted onto the finished sock.

SKILL LEVEL: Experienced
SIZE: U. S. 7.5 / European 38
YARN: CYCA #3 (DK/light worsted) Regia 6-ply
150 g / 375 m, 75% virgin wool / 25% polyamide
– Color A white (06860), approx. 95 g
– Color B burgundy (06046), approx. 15 g
CYCA #3 (DK/light worsted) Regia Active 6-ply
50 g / 125 m, 40% wool / 40% acrylic / 20% polyamide
– Color C apple green (05967), a small amount for crocheting the stems.
NEEDLES: Set of double-pointed needles, U. S. size 2.5 and 4 / 3 and 3.5 mm for stranded knitting; crochet hook U. S. size G-6 / 4 mm
GAUGE: 24 sts stockinette stitch on smaller needles / 24 sts stranded knitting on larger needles = 4 in. Adjust needle size to obtain correct gauge if necessary.

With Color A and smaller needles, cast on 60 sts (15 sts / needle) and join to work in the round. Begin Chart A; the pattern repeats 15 times per row. After completing Chart A, k 2 rows, change to larger needles, and begin stranded knitting following Chart B; the pattern repeats 6 times per row.

After completing Chart B, change to smaller needles and k 1 row with Color A. Work Chart C for 12 rows; the pattern repeats 6 times per row. K 3 rows with Color A and begin heel.

HEEL: Slip 1 st from Ndl 4 onto Ndl 3. The heel is knit back and forth across the 29 sts on Ndls 1 and 4. Knit the stitches on Ndl 1 onto Ndl 4 and turn work. Make a double stitch (= slip 1 st purlwise and pull the yarn so tight that the stitch turns around and it looks like you have two stitches on the needle). P28. Turn work. Make a double stitch and knit until the double stitch made on the previous row. Do not knit the double stitch. *Turn work. Make a double stitch and purl until the double stitch made on the previous row. Turn work. Make a double stitch and knit until the double stitch made on the previous row.* Repeat * to *, until there are 10 double stitches on both sides of the heel and you have just knit the middle 9 stitches.

Do not turn the work, but continue knitting 1 row around the sock as follows: k 10 double stitches, knit across Ndls 2 and 3, k 10 double stitches. The heel is now shaped like a triangle. Now we start lengthening the heel rows.

K9 and turn work. Make a double stitch, p8, turn work. *Make a double stitch, k until you reach the double stitch made on the previous row, k the double stitch, k1, turn work. Make a double stitch, p until you reach the double stitch made on the previous row, p the double stitch, p1, turn work.* Repeat * to * until you can make one last double stitch at the beginning of a right side row. Make the double stitch, k13. You are now at the new beginning of row. Continue to work in the round.

Knit until the double stitch made on the previous row. Knit the double stitch together with the 1st st on Ndl 2 and leave the stitch on Ndl 1. Knit until the last stitch on Ndl 3. Ssk this stitch and the double stitch on Ndl 4. Slip the stitch on Ndl 4 and knit across to the end of the row.

Continue to work stockinette stitch in the round. On every other row, k2tog at the end of Ndl 1 and ssk at the beginning of Ndl 4, until you have 52 sts. Divide the stitches equally across the needles (13 sts / needle.) Continue stockinette stitch until the foot measures 8 in / 20 cm or the pinky toe is covered. Begin toe decreases.

TOE DECREASES: At the end of Ndls 1 and 3, k2tog, k1. At the beginning of Ndls 2 and 4, k1, ssk. Work decreases every other row until every needle has 6 sts. Continue decreases on every row. With 12 sts remaining, cut yarn, pull through the stitches, and pull tight.

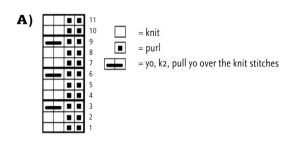

A)

☐ = knit
■ = purl
▭ = yo, k2, pull yo over the knit stitches

■ = purl

C)

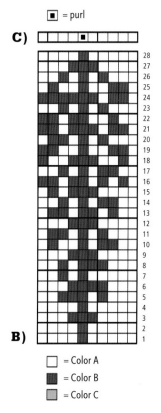

B)

☐ = Color A
■ = Color B
▨ = Color C

LUPINE STEMS: Use your green yarn to finish off the socks with crocheted stems. Start at the bottom and work your way up to the flower. The yarn is held at the back of the work. Push your hook through the 1st purl stitch and pull the green yarn through. *Skip over two horizontal bars and push the hook through to the wrong side. Pull the yarn to the right side and through the stitch on your hook.* Repeat * to * until you have completed the stem. Cut yarn and pull through the stitch on the hook and back to the wrong side from the outside of the stitch.

Weave in ends and steam press the socks lightly.

Many Thanks

TO MY SKILLFUL AND HARD-WORKING TEST-KNITTERS:

Marjo Huisman, Hanne Nybo, Susanna Latva-la-Andersson, Pirkko Karhu, Laura Meisalmi, Mona Tiirikainen, Eddie Fock, Minna Hietanen, Piia Laitala, Sasa Korteniemi, Julia Tuuhela, Hanne Jåfs, Anne Huittinen, Sonja Puskala, Ria Valjanen, Sari Ahlqvist, Riikka Kultalahti, Teija Merikallio, Anu Suokas, Minna Haataja!

Thank you to the models in this book: Pipsa Haavisto, Heini Paajanen, Bono, Baby, Kaaleppi!

I also want to thank my dearest friend Kaaleppi for his continuous and utter disinterest in my knitting projects. He helps me put things into perspective.

KAALEPPI·

Yarn Information

DROPS Garn Studio yarns are available from:

Garn Studio
www.garnstudio.com

Most Regia yarns, plus a variety of additional and substitute yarns, are available from:

Schachenmayr
www.schachenmayr.com

Laughing Hens
www.laughinghens.com

Wool Warehouse
www.woolwarehouse.co.uk

Black Sheep Wools
www.blacksheepwools.com

LoveKnitting.com
www.loveknitting.com

If you are unable to obtain any of the yarn used in this book, it can be replaced with a yarn of a similar weight and composition. Please note, however, the finished projects may vary slightly from those shown, depending on the yarn used. Try www.yarnsub.com for suggestions.

For more information on selecting or substituting yarn, contact your local yarn shop or an online store; they are familiar with all types of yarns and would be happy to help you. Additionally, the online knitting community at Ravelry.com has forums where you can post questions about specific yarns. Yarns come and go so quickly these days and there are so many beautiful yarns available.